PARSON, PRIEST AND MASTER
National Education in Co. Meath, 1824-41

Maynooth Studies in Local History

GENERAL EDITOR Raymond Gillespie

One of the features of the practice of Irish history in recent years has been the dramatic growth of interest in local and regional history. This has manifested itself in many ways. There have been a number of monographs dealing with particular national problems from a local perspective. Large collections of essays on local topics, usually based on the county, have been published. At the same time there has been a veritable explosion in the number of local historical journals and pamphlets, many available only at parish level. All of these publications have been important in awakening and fostering interest in the study of the local past but they are not without their problems. On the one hand they have tended to insist on the 'particularity' of places and on the other hand they often generalise from local studies to a national pattern.

This series of Maynooth Studies in Local History, whose origins lie in the St. Patrick's College, Maynooth M.A. course in local history instituted in 1992, presents local historical research which attempts another approach. The essays portray not 'particular places' but the experience of different groups of people or of individuals in the past. They explore the evolution of urban and rural communities in Ireland: how they organised themselves for day-to-day life and how they responded to pressures from within the community and to demands for change from regional or national forces.

It is intended to publish a number of studies every year which will focus on these problems from different chronological and geographical perspectives. Such studies will build up a picture of the varying communities of Ireland from the middle ages to the present day and in doing so present local history as the vibrant and challenging discipline that it is.

Maynooth Studies in Local History: Number 1

Parson, Priest and Master
National Education in Co. Meath, 1824-41

Paul Connell

IRISH ACADEMIC PRESS

Set in 10 on 12 point Bembo
and published by
IRISH ACADEMIC PRESS LTD
Kill Lane, Blackrock, Co. Dublin, Ireland
and in North America by
IRISH ACADEMIC PRESS LTD
c/o ISBS, 5804 NE Hassalo Street, Portland, OR 97213.

A catalogue record for this title
is available from the British Library.

ISBN 0-7165-2570-4

Printed in Ireland
by ßetaprint Ltd, Dublin.

Contents

Preface

It is with pleasure that I acknowledge my indebtedness to the following for their help and co-operation during the researching and writing of this study.

To Rev. Professor Donal Kerr for his initial encouragement and continuous support. To Professor Vincent Comerford and the teaching staff of the Department of Modern History, Maynooth College. In particular I would like to thank Ms. Mary Cullen and Dr. Raymond Gillespie for their invaluable guidance and assistance.

To the staff of the following institutions who were at all times extremely courteous and most helpful: The National Archives, Bishop Street, Dublin; The National Library of Ireland, Kildare Street, Dublin; Church of Ireland College of Education Library, Rathmines, Dublin; The Library, St. Patrick's College, Maynooth; Westmeath County Library, Mullingar, county Westmeath.

To my bishop, Dr. Michael Smith, bishop of Meath, and my colleagues in St. Finian's College, Mullingar, for making it possible for me to undertake this study.

Finally, I wish to thank my colleagues in the Maynooth M.A. in local history class of 1992-4.

Paul Connell
St. Finian's College, Mullingar

Introduction

The national education system transformed educational provision in the country over a period of some forty years. By 1871 there were over 7,000 national schools educating almost one million children. It was the earliest such national primary educational system in these islands and it became a model for other countries to follow. The textbooks published by the commissioners were used all over the English speaking world. From its foundation there was a steady decrease in the rate of illiteracy in the country. Although the Irish language was struggling before 1831 the national system accelerated its decline by refusing to recognise its existence even in the Irish speaking areas of the country.

The purpose of this study is to examine the early years of the national education system in county Meath. It will establish what kind of educational provision was in place in the county before 1831 and then trace the development of the new system in its first ten years up to 1841. The county is an appropriate way to study the system at a local level because it was the administrative unit favoured by the board especially in its early years. This study does not deal with matters like textbooks, syllabi and pupil achievement, because to do so properly would involve a much larger commitment than is possible for a work of this size. Instead, it will focus on the number and type of schools available and how they served the local community. In particular, it will look at the changes brought about in this regard by the new national system in its first ten years. In so far as possible it will attempt to link the schools with the local communities which they served.

Some work has been done on the national school system at a local level in recent years. These studies include Mary Daly's on the operation of the national system in counties Cavan, Cork, Kilkenny and Mayo in its first ten years, Harold O'Sullivan's on the emergence of the system in county Louth, and Sr. Mary Fahy's on the system in the diocese of Kilmacduagh.[1] In addition there have been a number of post graduate studies, including Patrick Kelly's in 1975 on the national system in Connaught, William Boyle's in 1990 on the system in county Donegal and most recently that of Claire Cotter in 1991 on the development of primary education in county Carlow.[2]

The sources available for a local study of the national system are both vast and yet limited. The new board was very strong on administration and there is a great wealth of material on local schools in terms of applications for aid, salary books, registers of correspondence and inspectors reports. The difficulty with this material is that a great deal of it reflects the priorities of the commissioners and does not, especially after the first two years, give a great deal of local perspective. As local records in the schools are almost non-existent this local perspective can only be patched together from other sources like parish histories.

The other major source for this topic are the numerous parliamentary papers relating to education. These are especially useful for the early years of the century, in particular the reports of the commissions of inquiry into educational provision between 1824 and 1828. Once again the difficulty with them is that they are looking at education to a great extent from a national perspective. Nevertheless they are very useful in helping to build a picture of a local area. This study does not make use of local newspapers as they are not very useful for the time frame involved. There are only two newspapers which span the period, the *Drogheda Journal* and the *Drogheda Conservative Journal*, and they contain very little local news.

Chapter one makes a detailed study of the educational returns from county Meath which were included in the second report of the commissioners of educational inquiry. They provide an amount of detail on the provision of schools in the county in the years 1824-5. The chapter begins by giving a background to the situation in the period 1824-5 and then goes on to deal with the returns in detail. It uses them to focus on the number and type of available schools, the cost of the buildings, the salaries of the teachers, and the number and religious denomination of pupils attending school. It also attempts to explain why educational provision was not uniform across the county.

Chapter two begins by looking at the background to the setting up of the national system and explains the regulations of the new board. It then shows the development of the system over its first ten years, looking at the applications for aid to the new board. It also deals with the number of national schools, enrollment figures and the salary of teachers. Finally it links the schools with the local community by looking at who the correspondents were for the new schools, what the reactions were on the part of local people to the new system, how the new schools affected existing schools and the level of continuity between the national schools and their predecessors.

Education in Co. Meath, 1824-5

On 9 March 1824 the Irish Catholic bishops through the auspices of Henry Grattan M.P. presented a petition to the House of Commons. This petition enumerated Catholic grievances on education, in particular the lack of financial support for Catholic schools, and the activities of Protestant proselytizing societies. Grattan told the House that he would move for a committee to investigate the distribution of Irish education funds.

> In the present state of Ireland, he prayed both the House and his majesty's government to weigh well the necessity of considering the condition of the great body of the people ... he would move for a committee to take into consideration the distribution of the funds appropriated to that object.[1]

The government's reaction to this petition was given in the House on 25 March. Sir John Newport moved that an address be presented to his majesty asking that he appoint a commission to investigate all aspects of Irish education including schools maintained in any part from public funds. The commission would report on measures for extending educational benefits to the people of Ireland.[2]

This royal commission sat from June 1824 to July 1827 and produced nine reports.[3] These publications were based on three types of evidence: statistical evidence provided by an extensive educational census, testimony and documents of assorted witnesses, and dealings with the Roman Catholic hierarchy. Although the commissioners did not solve the problems associated with Irish education, their nine reports did spur the administration in Ireland to take steps to solve the question. The eventual outcome was the setting up of the national education system in 1831.

The nine reports published by the commissioners are an invaluable source of information for the local historian. Of particular benefit is their countrywide educational census. The appendix to the second report of the commissioners lists schools in every parish of the country and provides a whole range of details concerning teachers, pupils in attendance and the state of schoolhouses.[4] This information was compiled in the autumn of 1824 when a circular form of return was sent to parochial clergy of both the Established and Roman Catholic churches. As a result two sets of figures were provided, one furnished by the Catholic priests and the other by the Anglican clergy. The person making the returns was required to 'verify them by swearing that he had inquired with due and reasonable diligence into matters contained in the returns and that the statement made therein was truth'.[5] The commissioners, on the basis of these figures, calculated that nearly twelve thousand schools countrywide were catering for some 560,000 children between 1824 and 1825.[6] But apart from giving an overall picture of education in the country these figures also make it possible to estimate the number of schools in any particular part of the country whether it be a parish, county, diocese or province. Using the information provided by the returns it is thus feasible to try and recreate the educational community in county Meath in the years 1824-5.

The returns give the location of each school within the county by townland and barony. They provide details on the name, religion and annual income of each teacher, followed by a description of the schoolhouse and in some instances its cost. The attendance figures for an average of three months are given for each school and the denomination and sex of the children. The figures sent in by the Catholic and Anglican clergy are placed side by side. Details are given of any aid the school was receiving whether from an education society or local patron. Finally the returns indicate whether scripture was read or not in each of the schools.

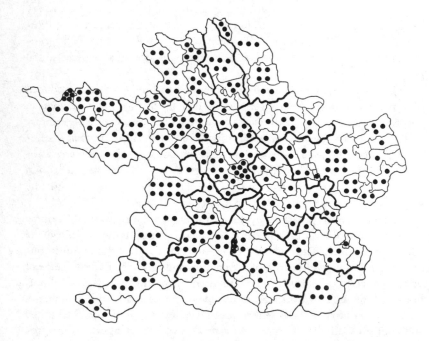

Figure 1.1 Schools in county Meath by civil parish 1824-5

According to the returns there were a total of 277 schools in county Meath in the period 1824-5. Figure 1.1 maps the distribution of these schools by civil parish. It shows that the schools were not evenly spread across the county. The baronies of Upper and Lower Deece, for example, have only a small number of schools. Table 1.1 lists the number of schools by barony and gives the population of each barony according to the 1821 census.[7]

	Table 1.1	
Barony	*No. of Schools*	*1821 Population*
Deece	10	8583
Demi-fore	25	12,671
Duleek	38	17,306
Dunboyne	6	2351
Kells	51	30,592
Lune	17	10,205
Moyfenrath	25	18,384
Navan	38	18,627
Ratoath	14	5391
Skryne	15	7979
Slane	38	27,094
Total	277	159,183

The largest number of schools are to be found in the baronies with the highest populations. However the ratio of schools to the 1821 population is not the same for all the baronies. Duleek has a ratio of one school to 400 people, while the equivalent figure for Slane is one school to 700 people. The distribution was also affected by the presence of a large town within a barony. The barony of Demi-fore contains twenty-five schools but eight of them are in the town of Oldcastle. The barony of Lune has seventeen schools with seven of them in the town of Athboy. In the barony of Navan there are thirty-eight schools but eight of them are in the town of Navan, and another nine are in the town of Trim. The barony of Slane has a population similar to that of Kells barony and yet has only thirty-eight schools as against fifty-one in Kells. Slane however had no large population centre unlike Kells where nine of the schools were in the town of Kells itself.

This figure of 277 schools compares favourably with counties of a similar population. The county of Waterford with a population of 156,521 had a total of 284 schools.[8] Before studying these returns in more detail it is worth looking at some developments and background in education in county Meath and the rest of the country up to 1825.

Like the rest of Ireland Meath had a strong tradition of interest in education. Sir Henry Piers writing in 1682 remarked:

> The people still retain an ardent desire for learning, and both at home and abroad do attain unto good measures thereof. There are from the highest to the lowest classes of them that are very ungenious and docile; in this unhappy, that they will not breed their youth in our universities, neither in this kingdom nor in England, because of the religion therein professed, but choose rather, being not permitted to have public schools of their own, to educate their children under private professors, or else send them abroad into France or Spain for their breeding. Neither is a priest now among them of any repute, if he has not spent some years abroad.[9]

With the accession of William III and the introduction of the penal laws, education for Catholics was forbidden at home and abroad under the severest penalties. Despite the penalties schools did manage to operate.[10] 'Popish schoolmasters' were hunted by the authorities and punished with the full rigour of the law: 'We present £10 ... to Capt John Odell for his service in taking Thomas Fitzgerald a popish schoolmaster.'[11]

Although there was some relaxation in enforcement from the 1750s it was not until 1782 that the laws banning Catholic education were changed. If a Catholic schoolmaster took the oath of allegiance to the Crown and got a licence to teach from the Anglican bishop he could do so.[12] When Dr. Patrick Plunkett, the Catholic bishop of Meath wished to have one or two schools in Navan he wrote to the Anglican bishop on 10 July 1783,

> The Roman Catholics of the diocese of Meath wish to avail themselves of the indulgence of the legislature, which, by a late Act, allows, under certain restrictions, persons of their persuasion to instruct youth in this kingdom. I am called upon by them humbly to request your Lordship will be pleased to grant the licence necessary for that purpose ... I should make it a capital object of my care that the Roman Catholic youth of this diocese should be taught to revere the civil constitution of their country, and that their affections should not be estranged from it by any unfriendly principles whatever...May I then presume to hope that, my Lord, that you will grant to one Roman Catholic, or more, if necessary, qualified as the law prescribes, a licence for teaching in Navan.[13]

The Anglican bishop replied that he would postpone a decision until he had an opportunity of discussing the matter in person with Bishop Plunkett.[14] A further Act of Parliament in 1792 dispensed with this provision of having to obtain a licence from the Anglican bishop.[15] Despite this, some type of licence was still necessary to establish that the other conditions of the 1782 Act were being complied with.[16] Few teachers however wished to draw attention to themselves and most schools in operation were illegal institutions until the passing of the Catholic Emancipation Act in 1829.

Bishop Plunkett showed a keen interest in education. He regarded it as essential to the further well being of the faith in Ireland. Ignorance he claimed had been the scourge of religion, whereas intelligence under proper direction would prove a valuable aid to the progress of the church. As a result of this the diocese of Meath had many schools before the Catholic relief bill of 1793.[17] On occasion he showed some disappointment that priests were not more zealous in their attitude to education.

> While the ministers of the established church, to their honour it may be said, in almost every part of the kingdom, were all alive to the importance and necessity of instructing youth, and taught schools themselves, it grieved me to the heart that many of us seemed to view that noble and most useful function without feeling or zeal – I had almost said with careless indifference.[18]

Bishop Plunkett in his decennial report to Rome in 1790 reported that there were 240 schools in the diocese despite the many difficulties placed in their way.[19] A close examination of his visitation records for the year 1788 makes possible a comparison with the parochial returns of 1824-5. In the Catholic parishes of county Meath he lists a total 107 schools.[20] This figure would not include Protestant schools, but by comparing it with only those schools which had Catholic teachers in 1825 it shows that the 1825 figure was an increase of over seventy per cent on that of 1788. Table 1.2 (*see next page*) makes a comparison between the 1788 figure and that of 1825. These figures do not take account of those parts of county Meath which are not in the diocese of Meath.

Catholics were prevented by law from teaching or operating schools but there were schools sanctioned by the state which Catholic children could attend. In theory, a network of schools existed to cater for all children. The origins and aims of these schools however did not endear them to the Catholic population. Parish schools had been established by parliament during the reign of Henry VIII. Every clergyman was bound by law to set up a school for teaching the English language and customs.[21] Diocesan schools were set up during the reign of Elizabeth I. Under an act of parliament each diocese was required to provide a free school with an English schoolmaster.[22] In

Table 1.2

Parish	1788	1825	Parish	1788	1825
Ardcath	3	5	Kilbeg	3	4
Athboy	5	7	Kilcloon	2	3
Ballinabrackey		4	Kildalkey	1	2
Ballivor		4	Kilskyre	3	3
Beauparc	2	4	Lobinstown	1	5
Bohermeen	2	6	Longwood		5
Carnaross	1	6	Moynalty	3	8
Castletown			Moynalvy	3	3
-Kilpatrick	2	5	Navan	3	6
Clonmellon	2	2	Nobber	4	6
Curraha	2	1	Oldcastle	5	8
Donore	3	2	Oristown	3	4
Drumconrath	2	4	Rathkenny	2	1
Duleek	3	7	Rathmolyon	4	6
Dunboyne	2	4	Ratoath	3	3
Dunderry	2	5	Skryne	3	8
Dunsany	3	2	Slane	2	4
Dunshaughlin	4	4	Stamullen	3	4
Johnstown	2	5	Summerhill	3	2
Kells	11	12	Trim	6	8

Total   107   182

1669 the Erasmus Smith schools were founded. Erasmus Smith was a London alderman who made a fortune in Irish land after the 1641 rebellion and in order to help secure title to these lands he made a grant of some of them for the foundation of Protestant schools. These schools were to propagate the Protestant faith using Ussher's catechism.[23] The last important foundation before 1782 was the charter schools. These schools were founded in 1733 by royal charter, as distinct from legislation, with the express purpose of combating Catholicism. Archbishop Boulter one of the founders of the Incorporated Society which ran these schools remarked in 1730 that 'the great number of papists in this kingdom and the obstinacy with which they adhere to their own religion occasions our trying what may be done with their children to bring them over to our church'.[24] Children were taken from their parents at an early age and housed, fed and instructed to the age of thirteen or fourteen. Edward Wakefield gives an account of one such school at Ardbraccan in county Meath which he visited in July 1808. He found a catechism in use containing the following questions and answers:

> Q. Is the church of Rome a sound and uncorrupt church?
>
> A. No, it is extremely corrupt, in doctrine, worship and practice.
>
> Q. What do you think of the frequent crossings, upon which the papists lay so great a stress in their divine offices, and for security against sickness and all accidents?
>
> A. They are vain and superstitious. The worship of the crucifix, or figure of Christ upon the cross is idolatrous, and the adoring and praying to the cross itself, is of all corruptions of the popish worship, the most gross and intolerable.[25]

Wakefield's account gives some indication as to why Catholics were reluctant to send their children to such schools.

The parish and diocesan schools by any standard were not successful. As the schools became identified as proselytizing agencies, Catholics grew reluctant to enroll their children.[26] Some 36,498 children were enrolled in 782 parish schools in 1823.[27] Of these 21,195 were Protestant children and 15,303 were Catholic children. By 1823 the population of the country was well over 6,000,000 and continuing to rise. The parish schools were not making any real impact on the bulk of this population.

With the lifting of most of the legal restraints on Catholic education in the latter part of the eighteenth century it was possible to create legally a network of schools acceptable to the Catholic population. However, neither the Catholic church authorities nor their people had the financial resources to build or fund such an enterprise. Catholics who wished to have their children educated were left with little choice. They could either send them to the existing Protestant schools or have them educated by the numerous hedge or pay schools that were to be found all over the country. These hedge or pay schools were the successors of the numerous illegal Catholic schools which had existed during the seventeenth and eighteenth centuries before the penal laws were relaxed. Fear of the law meant they had to be conducted secretly and out of doors as a householder was penalised for harbouring an illegal school.

> The schoolmaster selected in some remote spot, the sunny side of a hedge or bank which effectively hid him and his pupils from the eye of a chance passer-by and there he sat upon a stone as he taught his little school, while his scholars lay stretched on the green sward about him.[28]

Later when the laws against education were less strictly enforced, school was taught in a cabin, a barn or any building that might be given or lent for the purpose, but the name 'hedge school' was still retained. One of the earliest references to schools in Longwood, county Meath is contained in an undated piece composed by Watty Cox.

> When I was a boy, it was the custom of the artificial darkness of the period to study in thick bushes, but having a high conceit, a cabin kind of elevation of mind, I was taught in a large elm tree near Longwood, county Meath. It may be called the Tree of Knowledge, and I may now say with safety, as a compliment to our own happy times, it sometimes was not the Tree of Life; as we were not unfrequently disturbed in Reading Made Easy, by the growl of the bull-dog and the menace of the priest-hunter.[29]

When the Royal Commission on education issued its report on the parochial returns it did not mention the hedge schools as such. Instead they came under 'pay schools'. They defined 'pay school'.

> These schools cannot be considered as being under any particular superintendence. They arise from time to time, as circumstances create a demand for them; and are frequently undertaken by persons very ill qualified to discharge the duties of schoolmasters.[30]

The majority of children in school were attending these kind of schools. John Leslie Foster in a letter to the secretary of the Board of Education in 1811 stated that 'hardly any other country was so amply provided with the means of education. The people were taking education into their own hands and it was high time for the state to interfere.'[31] The government made no clearly defined gesture but it lent its support, and in some instances granted huge sums of money to Protestant education societies which appeared on the scene from the beginning of the nineteenth century. The prototype of these societies was the charter school society but as it had not achieved its aims a new effort was necessary.

The Association for Discountenancing Vice and Promoting the Knowledge and Practice of the Christian Religion was founded by three members of the established church in 1792. It made little headway until it received its first grant of £300 of government money in 1800. By 1823 this had risen to £9,084. The association gave money towards the establishment of schools and towards the payment of teachers. These schools were vested in the local church wardens and the Anglican minister. Teachers had to be Anglicans and all children had to read the scriptures. Catholic children were exempted only from the Protestant catechism. By the 1820s the association had become a vigorous proselytizing agency and as such was repugnant to Catholics who withdrew their children from the schools.[32]

Another of these societies was the Irish Society for Promoting the Education of the Native Irish through the Medium of their Own Language. This society based in London was founded in 1818 and had as its objective the promotion of scriptural education in Ireland using Irish as the medium of instruction. The society was merely using the language as the quickest route to the souls of the peasants. It provided funds for the purchase of bibles and there is evidence to show that it employed 'pay school' teachers in some areas.[33]

The most aggressive of the Protestant proselytizing societies was the London Hibernian Society which was founded in London in 1806. Its anti-Catholic principles cannot be in doubt.

> The great body of the Irish wander like sheep, that have no faithful shepherd to lead them ... The hope, therefore, that the Irish will ever be a tranquil and loyal people, and still more that piety and virtue will flourish among them, must be built on the anticipated reduction of popery.[34]

The society claimed a total enrollment of 61,387 in 1823.[35] The Catholic clergy were hostile from the beginning and a large number of Catholic children were withdrawn from the society's schools in the 1820s. It did not receive direct government grants but instead received subsidies from the Association for Discountenancing Vice.

It was also funded from the lord lieutenant's school fund.[36] This fund had been created in 1819 following an appeal on behalf of Catholics by William Parnell. Its purpose was to assist poor Catholics in erecting schools but the commissioners in charge of it made it very difficult for Catholics to get funds. They required considerable pledges of financial aid from local sources before making a grant and this requirement led to the rejection of many Catholic applications. It did not help that in order to receive aid schoolhouses had to be vested in the Anglican minister and church wardens of the parish. James Murray the parish priest of Clonmellon in county Meath made an application on 13 September 1825.

> To his Excellency Marquis Wellesly Lord Lieutenant General and General Governor of Ireland etc etc etc.
> That he has heard with great satisfaction that funds have been put into your Excellency's hands for the purpose of promoting Education.
> That in this parish situate partly in Meath, and partly in Westmeath there is a population of about four thousand persons.

That for the education of the younger portion of this population we
have six schools. All the school houses are in a wretched state. The
one in Clonmellon is in ruins.

And from the importance that your Excellency attaches to education, and from the want of means to promote it in this extensive
parish, your Memorialist feels a conviction that your Excellency will
take the premises into kind consideration.

Memorialist takes leave to add that this parish has been always peace-
able and that assistance afforded for the extension of Education will
be received with the greatest gratitude.

And Memorialist will pray.[37]

Fr. Murray did not receive any aid from the fund nor indeed did a
colleague of his, Fr. Michael Flood, parish priest of Kilskyre following a
similarly worded application on 15 September 1825.[38]

One society which was initially welcomed and proved successful in at-
tracting many Catholics was the Society for Promoting the Education of
the Poor in Ireland, otherwise known as the Kildare Place Society. Founded
in Dublin in 1811, its purpose was to educate the poor without any sectarian bias. The bible was to be read in its schools but without note or comment. From 1816 it received substantial government grants which by 1831
amounted to £30,000 annually. By that year it had aided over 1,600 schools
and educated through them 137,639 pupils.[39] When the society began to
co-operate with some of the other Protestant societies in the 1820s and
refused to change the composition of its management committee it was
heavily criticised by both the Catholic bishops and politicians of the stand-
ing of Daniel O' Connell. This criticism was part of the background to the
petition sent to parliament in 1824 by the Catholic bishops.

While the future national school system developed into a denominational system, it is not possible to distinguish in the returns which schools
were 'Catholic' and which were 'Protestant'. It is easier to label a school
'Protestant' as many of them were either parish schools or schools receiving
aid from a society which insisted on close links with the local Anglican
parish. Very few of the schools are described as connected with Catholic
parishes but given the interest of the clergy in education and the strong
opposition they gave to the proselytizing societies it is certain that there
were close links between the Catholic church and many of the 'pay schools'.
Mary Daly in her study of the early years of the national school system in
counties Cavan, Mayo, Cork and Kilkenny points out that

the impression which emerges (from the parochial returns) is that
active Catholic clerical involvement in education was restricted to
free schools commonly attached to Catholic chapels ... A closer ex-

amination of the available evidence suggests that this is a misleading impression. A significant number of the pay schools were in practice quasi-parish schools, receiving the patronage and perhaps the financial support of the local Catholic clergy.[40]

There is evidence to support this viewpoint in the applications made to the national board after 1831 from county Meath.[41]

At the request of the commissioners the religion of each teacher is stated in the returns. This study groups the schools on this basis because by so doing some interesting insights are provided into the educational community in county Meath in 1824-5. It would be wrong however, to make this an absolute demarcation because there is no way of establishing what links, if any, some of the schools had with either denomination. Even the returns made by the Catholic clergy show that some 146 schools out of 277 (fifty-three per cent) had at least some Protestant pupils.

Table 1.3 lists the number of schools by barony and distinguishes them by teacher denomination. The total number of schools listed in the returns for county Meath is 277. Five of these schools are not included in Table 1.3 because they had no teacher at the time the returns were collected. Seventy-seven per cent of the schools had Catholic teachers while twenty-two per cent had Protestant teachers.

Apart from religious denomination the schools can be divided into two main types. Twenty-eight of the schools were free schools where the children did not pay anything for their tuition. The remaining 243 were pay schools where the children paid at least some contribution towards their tuition. Over ninety per cent of the schools therefore were pay schools.

Table 1.3

Barony	No. of Schools	Protestant	Catholic	Mixed
Deece	10	4	6	
Demi-fore	25	5	18	2
Duleek	38	6	32	
Dunboyne	6	1	5	
Kells	51	9	42	
Lune	17	3	13	
Moyfenrath	25	5	20	
Navan	38	13	25	
Ratoath	14	3	9	
Skryne	15	3	12	
Slane	38	9	27	
Total	277	61	209	2

Fourteen of the free schools had Protestant teachers. They derived aid from a number of sources. Some like those in Kells and Dunboyne were parish schools supported by the local rector. Others like the two free schools in Athboy were supported by a local landlord, Lord Darnley. The Protestant free school in Trim was a charter school. While fourteen out of sixty schools with Protestant teachers were free schools (23.3 per cent), only twelve out of 209 schools with Catholic teachers were free schools (six per cent). This is a clear indication of how the Catholic population in the county was hindered in its attempts to provide education for its young people by inadequate financial resources. Catholic free schools were supported by subscriptions from the local parishioners. The Catholic free school in Navan, for example, was supported by an annual charity sermon.

Table 1.4 lists the number of schools in county Meath receiving aid from the various education societies in 1824-5.

Table 1.4

Society	Number	Protestant	Catholic
Assoc for Dis Vice	8	8	–
London Hib Soc	2	2	–
Irish Society	11	2	9
Kildare Place Soc	18	9	9
Total	39	21	18

Given the insistence on the part of the Association for Discountenancing Vice on having a Protestant teacher in all their schools it is not surprising that no school with a Catholic teacher in county Meath was receiving aid from that society. Although the London Hibernian Society did employ some Catholic teachers there were none in their two schools in the county.[42] The table shows that the Irish society was quite prominent in the county, subsidising teachers in nine Catholic schools. The schools like those in Nobber, Moynalty, Kilskyre and Bohermeen were located in areas of the county where the speaking of Irish was still common. The bishop of Meath Dr. John Cantwell wrote in 1834 that 'there are some good Irish scholars in the neighbourhood of Kells. It is the language spoken by the peasantry in that country.' A book preserved in the parish records of Moynalty, county Meath notes that: 'the Irish language is commonly spoken, the children understand it, but when they grow up they dont speak it. 'Tis likely to become extinct in a few more generations.'[43] Given that the Kildare Place Society was initially welcomed by Catholics the figures for the county are no surprise. Within a couple of years these schools were finding it difficult to stay open because of the withdrawal of Catholic children from them.

The patron of Knightstown school near Navan, Sir. J.M. De Bathe, wrote to the society on 4 February 1829 'The patron states that he cannot consistently with the desire he feels of benefiting his Roman Catholic peasantry continue the school in connection with the society.' He was writing following a report from the society's inspector who had called to the school only to discover that it was closed due to the opposition of the local priest.[44] Three years earlier the society had struck off Ratoath school because they had received a letter from the local parish priest stating 'that in consequence of a letter he received from his Prelate he cannot any longer comply with the regulations of the society.'[45]

One hundred and thirty described themselves as being in receipt of no aid of any kind. This figure is made up of eight schools with Protestant teachers and 122 schools with Catholic teachers. In all, forty-one schools are described as parish schools, thirty-eight of these having Protestant teachers and three having Catholic teachers. Also of interest is the presence of two boarding schools in the town of Navan. One was a pay school run by a Protestant lady and the other was the diocesan minor seminary – St. Finian's College. There was also in Navan a convent school run by Loreto sisters. One of the schools in Trim with a Protestant teacher was actually a school in the town gaol.

The two schools mentioned in table 1.4 which had both Catholic and Protestant teachers were located in Oldcastle. They were the result of an endowment set up by a gentleman called Laurence Gilson. A native of the town he had made a fortune in London. When he died in 1810 he had no issue and left £35,000 for the support of a school in Oldcastle to be run on the principles of Joseph Lancaster, a prominent English educationalist.[46] In 1825 as the school premises was not yet built the children were attending school in two separate buildings, one for boys and one for girls.

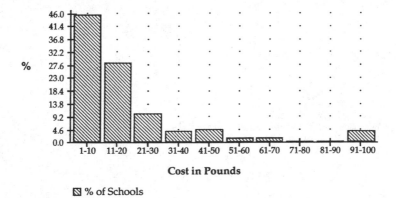

Figure 1.2 County Meath parochial returns. School buildings costs in £.

If there was variety in the type of schools in county Meath, there was an even greater variety in the type of building they were held in. There is a great deal of information in the parochial returns on the type of schoolhouses in the county and on their condition. Of the 277 schools 151 give details on the cost of construction. Out of these 151 schools 127 of them were built for £100 or less. Figure 1.2 (*previous page*) looks at these schools in more detail.

Figure 1.2 shows that of these 127 schools nearly eighty-four per cent cost £30 or less. Including all 151 schools the figure is seventy-one per cent. This is a clear indication of how basic school facilities were in the county. Some schools were well constructed. The pay school at Flower Hill in Navan run by Patrick Collessy and Rose Ludlow was made of lime and stone and was slated. It had cost £250 to build and catered for forty-four pupils. There are eight schools listed as costing £250 or more but with the exception of this school they are all charter or parish schools.

The charter school in Navan cost £1,100. The Catholic diocesan college of St. Finian's in Navan cost £4,000 but it was a boarding school catering for sixty-five pupils.

Figure 1.3 provides a breakdown of school cost based on the religious denomination of the teacher. While only fifty per cent of schools with Protestant teachers cost £30 or less the equivalent figure for schools with Catholic teachers is 93 per cent. The disparity in cost is even more obvious if the figure for schools costing £10 or less is used. While only 7.7 per cent of schools with Protestant teachers fit into this category, 55.4 per cent of schools with Catholic teachers do. These figures provide clear evidence of the scant financial resources available to Catholics to establish schools, unlike their Protestant contemporaries who were ably assisted by the government in various ways.

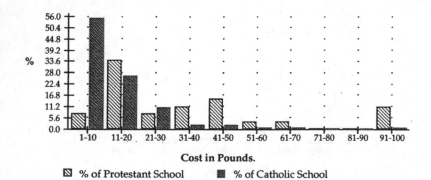

Figure 1.3 County Meath parochial returns.
School buildings costs in £, Catholic v. Protestant schools.

Apart from cost, there is a lot of information in the returns on the physical makeup of schoolhouses. Nineteen of the schools were listed as being held in the Catholic chapel while four were attached to a glebe or vestry. Eight schools were held either in a barn, stable or outhouse. Sixty-five of the returns use the word house to describe the building. Table 1.5 breaks these descriptions down.

Table 1.5 House type

mud	7	father's	2	market	2	stone	4
lodging	2	dwelling	10	alm	1	slated	5
rented	1	turf	1	gate	1	waste	1
glebe	2	thatched	26				

Forty-two of the returns describe the schoolhouse as being a cabin. A breakdown of these in Table 1.6 show that many buildings were little more than a makeshift shelter.

Table 1.6 Cabins

mud	14	thatched	5
bad	1	poor	3
miserable	4	wretched	3
common	1	small	8
stone			

The returns also look at the building materials used in the construction of these schools. Table 1.7 gives a breakdown of these.

Table 1.7 Building materials

Thatched	104	Slate	27
Lime	68	Stone	102
Mortar	13	Mud	73
Clay	9	Straw	4
Stone & lime	68	Stone & slated	22
Stone & thatched	37	Stone & mortar	12
Stone & mud	13		

Some of the returns give a very detailed description of the materials used in the construction of the schoolhouse, others less so. Table 1.7 lists the number of times a particular material was mentioned. Some of these figures are duplicates in the sense that a few of these materials may have been mentioned in any one return. They do however give a good indication of the type of construction used in these buildings.

Figure 1.3 showed the large disparity in cost between schools with Catholic teachers and those with Protestant teachers. The other information on school construction bears this out also. Out of a total of sixty schools with Protestant teachers twelve are described as built of stone and slated. Twenty-three are described as built of lime and stone. Out of 209 schools with Catholic teachers twelve are described as built of stone and slated, while only thirty-six mention a lime and stone construction. This is evidence indeed of the inability of the Catholic population to support a school system without some sort of aid.

Schools consist of more than brick and mortar however. The returns are a valuable source of information on the teachers who taught in, and the pupils who attended the schools in county Meath in 1825. The 277 schools in county Meath in 1825 had a total of 292 teachers. Of these, 221 were listed in the returns as Catholic, sixty-nine were listed as members of the established church and two were listed as Methodists. Seventeen per cent of all teachers were female, but while thirty per cent of the Protestant teachers were female only thirteen per cent of Catholic teachers were female.

The quality of teaching provided by these teachers is difficult to ascertain as the returns made no attempt to judge teaching standards. Later evidence from the applications for aid to the national board of education show that there was a wide divergence in standards.[47] Given the size of some of the schools and the poor quality of many of the schoolhouses this is not surprising.

Fr. John O'Connell the parish priest of Kildalkey wrote in the application form for a new national school in 1834 that:

> if Kildalkey school receives aid it would at once annihilate all the other wretched schools thro the parish, which on account of their cheapness, all poor children who go to school are obliged to resort to and from which they must derive the most worthless education.[48]

Not all the evidence is as condemnatory as this. Fr. Laurence Grehan looked back on his teacher with admiration and gratitude.

> I went occasionally to Mr. James George, who kept school in the Corrigeen and in various other places, and who occasionally came to my Father's house in capacity of private tuitioner, a name which

the preceptor himself used pronounce with singular self conceit. He was a peculiar man, he delighted in polysyllabic words; he fed on newspapers, carried them everywhere, read them in solitary bowers and at the pleasant fireside. He was equal to any problem in Goff or Vorster. No man could read faster. He was a fund of information, a really interesting man. This passing tribute I am bound to pay to one who taught me the use of the pen.[49]

Whatever about a general education, there is some evidence that the hedge schools did not promote the speaking of Irish. The teacher in the hedge school in Kilskyre, 'did his utmost to extirpate the speaking of Irish by his pupils, and it was a daily performance for him to inflict dire and punitive corporal punishment on any pupil who inadvertently or otherwise uttered an Irish word in his hearing'. [50]

This evidence may be merely an example of the dislike of one teacher for the language but it is in line with the view expressed by Akenson and others that while the later national school system contributed to the demise of the Irish language by not including it in its curriculum, the pattern of decline had already established itself beforehand.[51]

If the returns are not very enlightening on the quality of teaching in the schools in county Meath they do provide a good deal of evidence on teacher income. The respondents were asked to give an estimate of the income of each teacher. Only fifteen of the schools listed for county Meath failed to provide this information. Of those schools that provided the information, some gave the annual income of the teacher while the others outlined what the pupils paid the teacher each week for their schooling. If these weekly sums are multiplied by the number of pupils in the school it is possible to get an approximate annual income for most of the teachers in the returns. It is important to stress, however, that this cannot be totally reliable as enrollment varied throughout the year. Some of the pupils paid the master in food and fuel rather than in money. McDermott, a hedge school teacher in Kells, was paid in potatoes, flour, meal and turf.[52]

Finally, the income of the master was often supplemented by a free house or garden, or both. This was especially true of the parish schools and those schools aided by a local landlord. The Methodist teachers in the school in Kilskyre were paid £30 per annum with a house and a two acre garden. The teacher in Moorechurch, Duleek was given free board and lodging by Mr. Moore, a local farmer.

Apart from the fifteen schools which returned no teacher income there are four others whose teacher income is difficult to estimate. Three were boarding schools, like St. Finian's College in Navan. These give the amount paid by each student, but as this would include board and keep it is impossible to establish what sums were paid to the teachers. The fourth school is one of the Gilson schools in Oldcastle. While one of the schools gives a teacher income of £9 per year per teacher, the other one which has only one teacher mentions £120 along with other benefits in kind. Such a disparity between schools does not make sense and as a result it is better to exclude it along with the boarding schools from any general calculation.

Figure 1.4 looks at the annual income of teachers in 258 schools in county Meath in 1825. Teacher income varied enormously from school to school. The largest number of teachers (thirty-two per cent) were paid between six and ten pounds a year. This level of income seems very low especially when compared to other kinds of income. Peter Connell has shown that some cottiers on the Napper estates near Oldcastle were earning over £10 a year in the 1780s.[53] While some teachers were able to supplement their income with a free house or garden it is obvious that teaching was not a lucrative profession in the 1820s. Three quarters of these teachers were earning £20 or less.

The returns also show a large disparity in income between Catholic and Protestant teachers. This is illustrated in fig. 1.5.

There is a clear disparity in income between Catholic and Protestant teachers. Seventy-nine per cent of Catholic teachers have an income of £20 or less, but the equivalent figure for Protestant teachers is only sixty-one per cent. While 34.3 per cent of Catholic teachers have an income between £6 and £10 only 27.7 per cent of Protestant teachers have a similar income. The lower the point on the income scale the higher the percentage of Catholic teachers.

Teachers of pay schools had some difficulty trying to collect their fees. James Gibney, a Dublin carpenter, recalled his old teacher's problems in this regard.

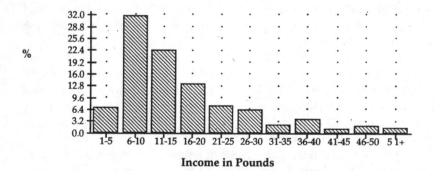

§ % of Teachers

Figure 1.4 County Meath parochial returns: teacher income, 1825

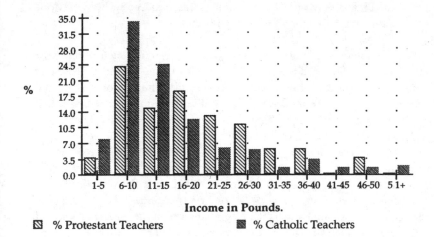

Income in Pounds.

◩ % Protestant Teachers   ▨ % Catholic Teachers

Figure 1.5 County Meath parochial returns: Protestant-Catholic teacher income

> My father rented, in my young days a small farm in the vicinity of Kells ... I was sent to school to Mc Dermott ... he had twenty four pupils, male and female, including his own two daughters...He had often great difficulty in making the parents of the children when their several quarter-year's tuition were up paying down the rhino for same, as they were mostly poor also; and when the stock of provisions in the bag was low he used publicly to read out in sharp tones the names of so and so, that were indebted to him, and that he wanted the money at once; at the same time pointing to his diminished bag. The pupils themselves, knowing when the bag was low, if their respective fathers were in debt for their tuition, were sure to ask them for the cash beforehand, and so prevent their names to be publicly announced in this manner.[54]

The life of a teacher was often filled with trials and disappointments and seemingly a great struggle for existence. Peter Galligan was probably the most famous hedge school master in county Meath in the early 1800s. He left behind a manuscript detailing what he taught and also a diary of where he taught over a twelve-year period from 1814 to 1825.

> My first commencement was in Ardamagh at Francis Flood's house on July 9th, 1814; next at Tom Lynch's near the bog, on the 1st February, 1815; then at Pat Muldoon's, 1st of May, 1815, continued there till October, 1816, then left off ... then removed to Owen Gearty's stable on Monday, 5th June 1820, and continued there till October following ... commenced again at widow Flood's, Ardamagh

on Thursday, May 24th, 1821 ... Commenced in Cruicetown Monday, 18th April, 1825 for twelve months.[55]

This is interesting evidence which depicts an educational system that was in constant flux. Galligan is listed in the parochial returns as master of Tawis school near Kilmainhamwood. He gave his annual income as £6 and the schoolhouse is described as a stone wall cabin worth £5. It is said that he never taught again after being denounced in 1826 by Fr. Halpin the parish priest of Moynalty for his connection with the Irish Society.

The returns provide very little information on pupils apart from giving attendance figures for most of the schools. Pupils are categorised by religious denomination and by sex. A major difficulty is the disparity in the figures between the Anglican and Catholic returns. Some schools have only one set of returns, while others fail to give the sex of the children. Some of the figures for attendances can be described no doubt as armchair statistics. As in all surveys of this nature there are bound to be inaccuracies. Many schools may have not been forthcoming if the questions were coming from a representative of the wrong denomination. A more likely reason for the disparity in figures is that the schools were visited at different times by each clergyman and the attendances may have varied on those days.

Figure 1.6 County Meath baronies 1824–5: pupil enrollment

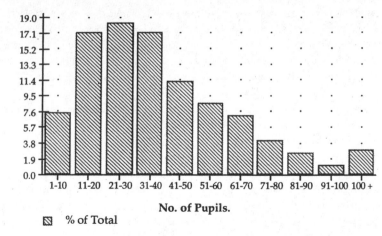

No. of Pupils.

☒ % of Total

Figure 1.7 County Meath parochial returns: pupil attendance figures

The Anglican returns give a figure of 8,899 children attending schools in the county. Of these 1,197 were Protestant children while 7,702 were Catholic or 13.5 per cent Protestant children and 86.5 per cent Catholic children. The Anglican returns go on to achieve a remarkable piece of mathematical gymnastics by listing 5,756 males and 3,191 females, which in effect gives a total pupil number of 8,947. The Catholic returns on the other hand give an attendance figure of 14,632, which is broken down into 1,187 Protestant and 13,445 Catholic pupils. The percentages are 8.1 per cent and 91.9 per cent. Not all the Catholic returns give a male and female breakdown, but of those that did 6,379 pupils were male while 3,529 were female. The divergence in the two sets of figures is interesting. There is only a difference of ten pupils between the two sets of figures for Protestant pupils, while there is a huge discrepancy of 5,743 for Catholic pupils. Given the large number of schools with Catholic teachers, the Anglican clergy were probably bound to get their figures wrong. It may reflect a desire on their part to underestimate the problem. The Catholic clergy may have been exaggerating numbers for effect but this is unlikely considering the potential Catholic school going population.

The 1821 census figures are not the most reliable, because of the way they were collected.[56] Allowing for this, and the fact that the population was rapidly increasing in the 1820s it is still interesting that this census states that there were 40,195 children in county Meath between the ages of five and fifteen.[57] Figure 1.6 gives the 1821 census figures for each barony in the county and places beside it the pupil enrollment figures as found in the Catholic returns along with the percentage of the census figure for 5-15 year olds that each represents. Even taking these larger totals from the Catholic returns it is clear that the schools in the county were educating only 14,632 pupils, a third of what would be the potential school going population in 1821. The figures for free education are even more stark. The twenty-eight free schools in the county, both Catholic and Protestant were educating at most 1,458 pupils. When the Catholic bishops were pointing out to the government of the day the great need for education aid they were not exaggerating.

Figure 1.7 looks in detail at pupil numbers in the 267 schools in county Meath who gave attendance figures in the returns. Just over half the schools in the county (52.8 per cent) had attendance figures of over eleven and less than forty pupils. The largest group of schools had attendance figures of between twenty-one and thirty pupils. According to the returns these figures represented an average attendance over the previous three months. It is important to note once again that attendance figures varied considerably depending on the season. During harvest time for example, attendances were especially poor for reasons of necessity at home.

As in the case of teacher income and school cost there is a marked disparity between schools with Protestant teachers and those with Catholic teachers. Figure 1.8 looks in some detail at this disparity. Unlike teacher income where the larger percentages are found in the schools with Protestant teachers, the opposite is the case here. Pupil numbers in schools with Catholic teachers are larger than in those with Protestant teachers. While 58.1 per cent of schools with Protestant teachers have enrollment figures of less than thirty pupils, the equivalent figure for schools with Catholic teachers is 39.3 per cent. In schools with Protestant teachers the largest percentage have enrollment figures of between eleven and twenty pupils. Schools with Catholic teachers, however, have the largest percentage in the thirty-one to forty pupil category. When these figures are used with school type and description they paint a grim picture indeed. The schools with the least resources were educating the larger number of pupils.

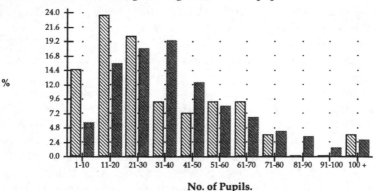

No. of Pupils.

◩ % of Protestant Schools   ◪ % of Catholic Schools

Figure 1.8 County Meath parochial returns: attendance,
Protestant v. Catholic schools

Since the reading of scripture was a contentious matter for the Catholic bishops the commissioners tried to establish in the returns how many schools held scripture reading during class time. Out of sixty schools with Protestant teachers in county Meath only four did not read scripture. Of those who did, forty-seven schools used the authorised version of scripture, one used the Douai version, while three schools used both versions. Three others schools read an unspecified version in Irish. The two remaining schools did not say which version they used. Considering the attachment of the Protestant churches to scripture reading it is not surprising to find ninety-three per cent of the schools with Protestant teachers reading scripture.

The schools with Catholic teachers were not so attached to scripture reading. Out of 212 schools only forty-four, or twenty-one per cent read scripture. Of those that did, eleven used the Douai version, with nineteen using the authorised version. Six schools used both versions. Another seven read an unspecified in Irish. One school did not say which version it used. It is interesting to note that while only one school with a Protestant teacher used the Douai version, nineteen schools with Catholic teachers used the authorised version. Five of these schools were aided by a local landlord or the Kildare Place Society. Just as the Douai version of scripture was anathema to Anglican clergy, the authorised version would not have been approved of by the Catholic clergy. A possible explanation might be that only Protestant pupils read scripture in those schools.

Many of the schools which did not read scripture taught catechism. Even the Kildare Place schools which were supposed to have no religious imput apart from the reading of scripture with no comment, had difficulty in excluding catechism from their schools. Time and time again the inspectors of the society reported the use of catechisms in defiance of the rules. The inspector visited Stamullen school on 4 May 1824 and reported back to the committee – 'Scripture not read, catechism taught.'[58] Ballymacglasson school was struck off the society's books on 22 April 1824 for breaching the scripture rule and teaching catechism.[59]

The Catholic clergy in the county were very active in tackling anything they saw as detrimental to the faith of their flock. The whole issue of proselytism was as much a local concern in county Meath as it was a national one for the bishops. A school at Charlesfort in Bohermeen parish met with spirited opposition from the local parish priest Fr. Michael Branagan. The school had been founded by a local landlord Mr. Tisdall who justified his establishment of it by issuing a pamphlet attacking the Catholic religion. Fr. Branagan replied in August 1823:

> It is said that there is an advertisement on the inside of the door of your schoolhouse, threatening any person who enters or disturbs the school, with a prosecution at law ... you have threatened your ten-

antry with vengeance, and to turn your poor labourers out of employment if they do not send their children to your school ... You
say you have no object in view but the good of your neighbours.
Prove this by your actions; ameliorate the conditions of your tenants
and labourers, and leave the choice of the school books and the
moral instructions to the pastors, who, without disparagement to
your talents are as well qualified to decide on such matters as your-
self, and then the tenantry shall cheerfully attend your school. I know
your tenantry well, and with the exception of two or three, I dont
know a poorer; and in my opinion you would benefit them more by
giving reasonable abatements in their rents than by distributing your
bibles, of which, if I am not misinformed, you have cart-loads in
your house this long time past ... I have in my possession The Advo-
cate of the Primitive Church, a book of dangerous tendency ... put
into the hands of one of my parishioners; and to induce the poor
man to swallow its contents with more ease, a sack of potatoes was
sent after it as a present.[60]

One of the schools attached to the Irish Society was located in Kilskyre
but it ceased to be connected to it in 1827 after charges of proselytism were
made against it. The teacher declared that:

he taught occasionally about five persons, one of whom was a Protestant; that he produced a larger number than he taught ... that he
did not wish to belong further to the Irish society, as he is of the
opinion that by so doing, he would act contrary to propriety and
conscience.[61]

A similar withdrawal from the Irish Society occurred in Moynalty after
strong opposition from the parish priest.[62] In Nobber, the parish priest Fr.
Halpin turned the parents of an Irish Society Inspector named Farrelly out
of the chapel because he was a 'devil incarnate, and a bible reading rascal'.[63]
Not all Protestant teachers were involved in proselytism. Fr. Laurence Grehan
attended a classical school in Trim and he later wrote about his experiences
there.

There were two brothers. One taught English and science; the other
taught Latin and Greek. They belonged to the Protestant religion;
yet they taught the Roman Catholic catechism, and often slapped
the younger lads when not answering correctly according to the
very words of the catechism ... they were respectable men of their
class and never presumed to interfere with the religious persuasion of
their pupils, half of whom were Catholic and half Protestant.[64]

Apart from scripture, the parochial returns provide no insight into the school curriculum. Other contemporary sources, however, are more enlightening. Peter Galligan's manuscript contains a great deal of information on the kind of subjects he taught.

> The contents of his manuscript form a sort of encyclopaedia of general, useful and sometimes valuable information. There are extracts from English literature, prose and poetry, numerous Irish poems and translations from Irish, verses on a variety of subjects ... In history there are translations of portions of Keating, and long extracts from Leland's 'History of Ireland'. There are notes on geography, astronomy, mathematics and philosophy. Arithmetic gets special mention ... In addition there is a quantity of eminently practical information: household and medicinal remedies, diseases of cattle and sheep and their remedies, legal advice and copies of wills ... and marriage notes.[65]

It appears that Peter Galligan provided a number of services for the local community apart beyond teaching.

A second parliamentary report, that of the Commission of Public Instruction for Ireland, which was published in 1835 gives details of schools in all the Protestant parishes of the country. The returns from this report give some information on what was taught in each school. Two schools listed both in the parochial returns and the 1835 report and who still had the same teacher were the chapel school in Trim and a school in Grangegeeth. Given that each had the same teacher in the years 1824-5 and 1835 it is more than likely that the curriculum did not change over the years.

The Trim school run by Philip Reilly was a free school supported by a chapel committee. It taught 'Reading, writing, arithmetic, bookkeeping, geometry, mensuration, and Roman Catholic catechism.'[66] In 1825 the enrollment was fifty-nine, but by 1835 this had risen to 252. The Grangegeeth school was run by Patrick Powderly and taught Reading, writing, arithmetic, bookkeeping and Roman Catholic catechism.'[67] By 1835 its enrollment had risen from thirty-eight to 117. A detailed study of the 1835 report shows a similar curriculum in operation in most schools.

The parochial returns give a very detailed description of schools in county Meath in 1825. It is important however to remember that schools were not separate entities in themselves, but were part of the wider community and indeed were shaped by it. The health of the local economy determined the extent to which the local community could invest in the education of their children. There is a good deal of evidence that there was a changing relationship between the population and the economy in the pre-famine decades in county Meath. Peter Connell has shown that there were definite

regional variations in the county.[68] While some areas stayed with either
tillage or grazing, others changed tack at various times to suit market trends.
This of course had serious repercussions for the population because while
tillage was labour intensive, grazing was not. T. Jones Hughes points out
that rural poverty was most in evidence in the tillage areas of the county
which had high population densities.[69] Peter Connell shows how landlords
in some areas of the county reacted to market trends and began to switch to
grazing in the 1820s. It was a trend noted indeed by the Halls, those intrepid
travellers of the 1830s. 'The clearing of estates has been proceeding at a
disastrous rate in Meath.'[70] This policy only accentuated the problem of
rural poverty in parts of the county.

The parochial returns show a definite connection between the health of
the local economy and the provision of schools. This is clear from a study of
two areas of the county with a similar number of schools. The barony of
Moyfenrath in the south west of the county had twenty-five schools. Taken
as a unit the baronies of Dunboyne-Ratoath in the south east of the county
had a total of 20 schools. The population of Moyfenrath according to the
1821 census was 18,384 while that of Dunboyne-Ratoath was 7,742. The
difference in population is explained by the fact that while Dunboyne-
Ratoath was a long established grazing area providing meat for the Dublin
market, the barony of Moyfenrath had a mixture of grazing and tillage and
a pronounced shift to grazing was establishing itself here in the 1820s.

Moyfenrath had a total school enrollment of 968, while that of Dunboyne-
Ratoath was 828. Apart from the obvious disparity in population an even
bigger one emerges when the 1821 census figures for children between the
ages of five and fifteen are taken into account. Here the figure for Moyfenrath
is 4,834 which indicates that the schools were educating only twenty per
cent of eligible children. In Dunboyne-Ratoath on the other hand the fig-

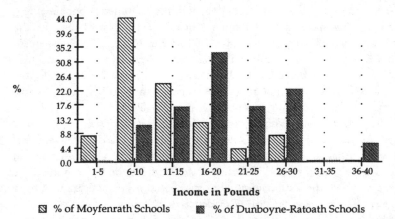

Figure 1.9 Teacher income: Moyfenrath barony v. Dunboyne-Ratoath baronies

ure was 1,168 which means its schools were catering for seventy per cent of
its eligible children. The same disparity appears when a comparison is made
of teacher income. Figure 1.9 looks at this in detail. While seventy-six per
cent of teachers in Moyfenrath have an income of £15 or less, only 27.8 per
cent of teachers in Dunboyne-Ratoath have incomes of this level. The
largest group of teachers in Moyfenrath (forty-four per cent) have an income of between £6 and £10. The largest group of teachers in Dunboyne-
Ratoath (33.3 per cent) have an income of between £16 and £20.

This variation between the two areas is re-inforced in other ways. Only
seven schools in the Dunboyne-Ratoath area are listed in the returns as
receiving no aid. All the other schools are aided either by the parishes in
question, two local landlords or by the Kildare Place Society. Education
societies, like that of the Kildare Place, never gave aid unless a substantial
amount of local aid was contributed. The local population had the resources
to provide this seed money. In Moyfenrath however, out of twenty schools
with Catholic teachers only one was receiving aid, from a local landlord.

What emerges from the parochial returns is a picture of a community
trying to provide education for their children with the very limited resources at their disposal. Some elements within that community had substantial resources but they did not offer them to the bulk of the population
without strings being attached. The Catholic population made valiant efforts to cater for the educational needs of their young people but were not
willing to do so at the price of endangering their faith. County Meath
confirms at a local level the fears and difficulties in the field of education
being expressed by the Irish bishops at a national level. What the parochial
returns also show is that although the county can be looked at as a conven-
ient unit of administration there were remarkable regional variations within
the county based on the type and health of the local economy.

The Development of the National School System in Co. Meath, 1831-41

On 9 September 1831, Edward Stanley, the Irish chief secretary, spoke to the House of Commons on the subject of Irish education.[1] The house was discussing a motion to grant a sum of £30,000 to enable the lord lieutenant to assist education in Ireland. Mentioning various parliamentary reports on Irish education from 1812 to 1830 he gave a history of the education grant to the Kildare Place Society and outlined the reasons why it was no longer suitable as the major recipient of government education funds. He proposed that £30,000, the amount voted in the previous year to the Kildare Place Society and the Association for Discountenancing Vice, be placed at the lord lieutenant's disposal. A board was to be created, partly Catholic, partly Protestant, to oversee the direction of schools in Ireland. After debating the matter, the motion was agreed to by the house.[2]

Stanley immediately set about creating the new board. In consultation with the lord lieutenant, Lord Anglesey, the duke of Lenister was made chairman of the board. Six other members were then appointed. They were Richard Whately, the recently appointed Anglican archbishop of Dublin, Daniel Murray, the Catholic archbishop of Dublin, Francis Sadleir, the provost of Trinity College, James Carlile, a minister of the Presbyterian church of Mary's Abbey in Dublin, A.R. Blake, a treasury official, and Robert Holmes, a Dublin barrister. Three of these were Anglican, the duke of Lenister, Archbishop Whately and Sadleir. Two were Catholic, Archbishop Murray and Blake and two were Presbyterian, Carlile and Holmes.[3] Stanley wrote to the duke of Leinster outlining what was expected of the new board.[4] The commissioners were authorised to disburse an annual grant from the lord lieutenant to help existing, and found new schools. The schools were to be non-denominational, but not secular. Four or five days each week were to be set aside for combined moral and literary instruction, and the remaining one or two days on a suitable time before or after combined instruction for separate religious instruction. Responsibility for religious education was given to the clergy of various denominations, who were permitted to hold classes for that purpose in schools at the appropriate periods. They also had control over books used for that purpose.

To promote mixed education as effectively as possible, Stanley's letter laid down that the board would probably look with 'peculiar favour' on applications for aid made jointly by the Protestant and Catholic clergy of the parish, from the clergy of one denomination and members of another, or from parishioners of both denominations. An application bearing the signatures of representatives of only one denomination would be scrutinised to discover why the other religious persuasion was not represented. A register was to be kept in every school outlining the attendance or non-attendance of each child at divine worship on Sundays. This stipulation about the keeping of such a register was later dropped at the request of the new board.[5]

Stanley also laid down certain conditions that had to be satisfied before aid was granted to a school, such as local provision of a permanent salary for the master, of furniture and repairs, of books, and of one third of the building costs. These instructions were later promulgated by the commissioners in their annual reports:

> Before such aid can be granted, the commissioners must be satisfied that the case is deserving of assistance, that there is reason to expect that the school will be efficiently and permanently supported; that some local provision will be made in aid of the local teacher's salary, either by school fees or otherwise; that the school-house is in good repair, and provided with a sufficient quantity of suitable furniture ... to entitle a school to a continuance of aid, the school-house and furniture must be kept in sufficient repair by means of local contributions.[6]
>
> Before any grant is made towards building a school-house, the commissioners are to be satisfied that a necessity exists for such a school, that an eligible site has been procured ... and that the applicant parties are prepared to raise, by local contribution, at least one third of the whole sum which the commissioners deem necessary for the erection of the school-house, providing furniture, etc.[7]

The patron or manager of a local board school was empowered to appoint and, if necessary, to dismiss teachers, though the board could also in exceptional circumstances call for a teacher's removal. He could also select the books for combined instruction but the commissioners had to sanction their use. The books for religious instruction had to be sanctioned by the members of the board who belonged to the same religious denomination as those for whom they were intended. The board later made available their own textbooks at reduced prices to existing schools and free to new schools, and the price and quality of these ensured their widespread use.

With the establishment of the national system of education all state assistance to other societies ceased. The commissioners held their first meeting on 1 December 1831 and appointed Thomas F. Kelly to be secretary to the board. They began receiving applications for aid almost immediately. The first four grants, amounting to £525 were issued on 19 January 1832.[8] At first, all applications for aid came directly to the combined board, but after a while a special sub-committee was appointed to do the investigative work. A great deal of care was put into the processing of applications and details about the applicants, land, sites and local resources were carefully checked. Among the new rules adopted was the stipulation that the two words 'national school' were to be inscribed on all buildings supported by the board.[9]

The establishment of the new board marked the beginning of a new era in the history of Irish education. The task of the commissioners was not an easy one. They had to face attacks by their co-religionists and were subjected to the close scrutiny of three official inquiries, one by the House of Lords in 1837, one by the House of Commons in 1837, and one by the select committee on foundation schools in Ireland which sat from 1835 to 1838.[10] As a board the commissioners had the ability and courage to make decisions on many fronts and to implement them with some expedition. The measure of their success can be judged by the fact that the system which they began in 1831 was by 1871 running almost 7,000 schools with nearly a million children on the rolls.[11] All this took time, but nevertheless even during the first decade a great deal was achieved.

The first application for aid to the new board was made on 10 February 1832 by the free school for the education of the poor in Navan. The correspondent was the Rev. Eugene O'Reilly, the parish priest of Navan. He was no stranger to the promotion of education having being president of the diocesan college of St. Finian in Navan from its foundation in 1802 to his appointment as parish priest of Navan in 1827. The application was signed by nineteen Protestants and twelve Catholics. The local Anglican clergy refused to sign the application as they disapproved of the new system. Fr. O'Reilly remarked in the application that there were over 500 children in Navan too poor to even pay a penny a week towards their education and they were all Catholic. A new school was being built for the female pupils and £200 in aid was being sought to finish it. He also requested a sum of £80 for 'the salaries of the masters and mistresses in the remote parts of the parish. Thus the poor of the parish will receive the benefits of a moral and religious education'.[12] The total cost of the new school was estimated at £600 but the application stated that an individual had donated £500. The commissioners granted £100 towards the cost of the school and £15 towards the salary of a teacher for the existing school. Fr. O'Reilly later made another application for aid for the female school and received a further £15 for salary purposes.[13]

Within a year eleven schools were receiving aid from the new board. Three of these schools, in Navan, Duleek and Ratoath, were separate female schools in the same location as the male school. Five of the schools were in rural areas, Clonard, Dangan, Donore, Fraine and Killeen.[14] By

1841 the number of schools attached to the board had grown to 78. Table 2.1 shows the growth over a ten year period.

The commissioners did not publish any statistics for national schools until 1835. The figures up to 1835 shown in fig 2.2 are based on the applications for aid to the commissioners, thereafter the official report figures are given.[15] These figures show a period of constant growth, the 1841 figure being a 278 per cent increase on that of 1835. The national growth for the

Table 2.1 *Number of schools*					
Year	Nationally	Co. Meath	Year	Nationally	Co. Meath
1831		0	1837	1300	35
1832		11	1838	1384	39
1833		19	1839	1581	52
1834		23	1840	1978	58
1835	1106	28	1841	2337	78
1836	1181	32			

same period is 211 per cent. There is a marked dip in the rate of growth in the year 1839. While there is no direct evidence available as to why this is the case it is interesting that this coincides with the dispute between the Irish bishops about the national system.[16] Bishop Cantwell of Meath was allied to those who wished Rome to condemn the system. With the settlement of the issue in 1840 some applicants may have felt more comfortable in applying for aid to the board.

By 1841 these seventy-eight schools had a total enrollment of 8,517 children. Of these 4,797 or fifty-six per cent were male and 3,720 or forty-four per cent were female. This is in line with the national figures for 1841

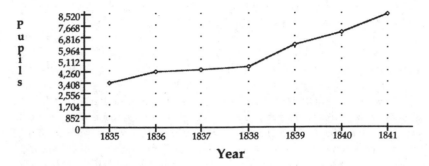

Figure 2.1 Meath national school enrollment, 1835-41

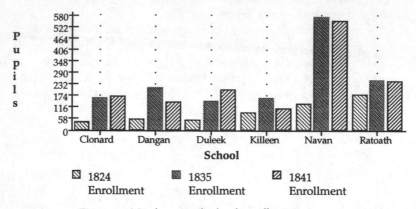

Figure 2.2 Meath national school enrollment, 1824-41

which were 56.6 per cent male and 43.4 per cent female. Figure 2.1 outlines the growth in pupil numbers in the schools between 1835 and 1841. Figure 2.2 gives the enrollment figures for nine national schools which were in existence as pay schools in 1824.[17] For this purpose the male and female schools in Duleek, Navan and Ratoath have been amalgamated.

The small decline in enrollment from 1835 to 1841 that is evident in some of the schools may have been due to the opening of other national schools in their area.

While there was a steady growth in enrollment during the period 1831–41 there was a substantial number of children not being catered for by national schools in the county in 1841. The 1841 census figure for persons under seventeen in county Meath was 77,785.[18] Allowing for the fact that some of these would have been too young or old to attend school, an enrollment figure of 8,520 represents only a small percentage of the total potential school going population. This fact is further borne out by the first report of the Royal Commission on the state of religious and other public instruction in Ireland. This report published in 1835 estimated that there was a total of 223 schools in county Meath, and of these, twenty-three were national schools. The total enrollment in these schools was 13,694 pupils, of whom 2,583 or nineteen per cent were attending national schools.[19] It is important to remember however, that when these figures were gathered by the commission the national system was barely two years in operation.

What is immediately obvious from fig. 2.3 is that the national schools are not evenly spread across the county. The greatest concentration of schools are in the baronies of Duleek, Ratoath, Lower Kells and a combination of Navan Lower and the northern area of Skryne. Some baronies like Fore and Upper Deece contain no national schools. Others like Upper Navan and Lower Slane contain only one national school. Remarkably the barony of

Upper Kells contains only three national schools, all in the western end of the barony. This is surprising as the 1841 census lists Upper Kells as having a total population of 22,142, the largest concentration of people in the county.[20]

There is an explanation for the lack of national schools in some baronies. It was not that applications for aid had been made and were turned down by the new board. In fact very few of the applications made to the board in the first nine years were refused. Rather it had to do with local conditions. In the barony of Fore, for example, there was an existing free school set up by the Gilson trust which was catering for 1,024 pupils in 1835.[21] Enrollment in this school was rising every year and there were plenty of funds available to meet the demand. The small number of schools in the Kells area can perhaps be explained by the fact that the parish priest there, Fr. Nicholas McEvoy was the archdeacon of the diocese and thus second only to the bishop. He was probably reluctant to apply for aid to the new board until the dispute among the Irish bishops over the system was resolved. The fact that he was an ardent nationalist who later became heavily involved in the repeal movement may have also coloured his approach. By 1847, however, he had applied for aid to the board for four schools in Kells.

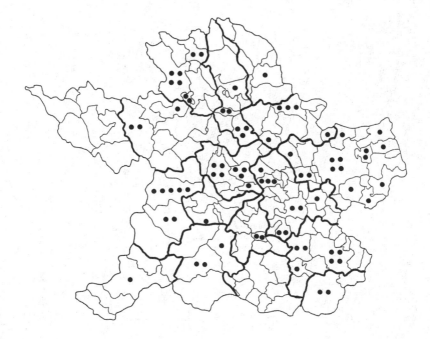

Figure 2.3 Distribution of national schools in county Meath, 1841

Another factor which affected the spread of national schools in the county was economic difference. One of the regulations that had to be satisfied by applicants for aid was that one third of the cost of a school had to be provided by the local area. Chapter one highlighted the economic differences between areas of the county. Moyfenrath barony had few aided schools in the 1820s unlike the more prosperous baronies of Dunboyne and Ratoath. The difficulty lay in the provision of matching local aid. It is interesting that the pattern is similar for national schools. Figure 2.3 shows that the less populated and more prosperous baronies of Dunboyne and Ratoath have nine national schools by 1841 whereas the combined baronies of Upper Deece, Upper and Lower Moyfenrath have only five. The 1841 census gives a population figure of 8,937 for Dunboyne-Ratoath, while that for Upper Deece and Moyfenrath is 26,664.

Figure 2.4 attempts to find a pattern to the location of national schools in the county. The schools are grouped together into three periods, depending on when they were established. The county had twenty-eight national schools in 1835. By 1839 it had another twenty-eight national schools. In the two years up to 1841 a further twenty-five were added. This total of eighty-one schools, includes three schools at Slane, Clonard and Dangan which did not persevere. Dangan and Clonard were separate female schools

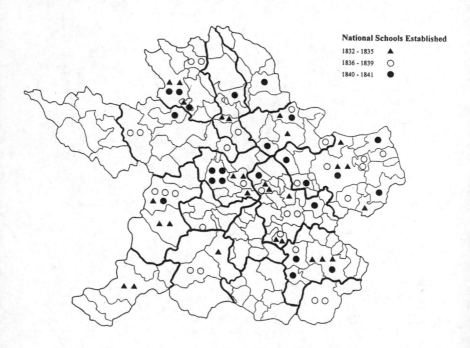

Figure 2.4 National schools established, 1832–41

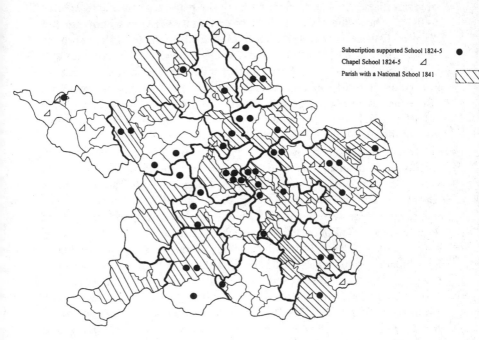

Subscription supported School 1824-5   ●
Chapel School 1824-5   △
Parish with a National School 1841   ⧄

Figure 2.5 Type and distribution of schools in county Meath, 1825-41

which re-amalgamated into the male schools. Slane was struck off in 1839 and rejoined the system in 1845.

As was clear in fig 2.3 the schools are clustered in particular areas of the county. However, by splitting them into three periods it is possible to see that new national schools tended to be established either in the same parishes as existing schools or in the adjoining parishes. The success of one venture obviously encouraged the establishment of another.

A study of the applications for aid re-inforces this idea. Six priests in the county were responsible for the establishment of twenty-four schools. Fr. Eugene O'Reilly, the first applicant to the board from county Meath, was responsible for the establishment of seven national schools in the Navan area. Fr. Matthew O'Hanlon the parish priest of Duleek was the correspondent for four national schools in his parish. Fr. Joseph Kennedy the curate in Bohermeen established four national schools in the area in 1841.[22] Mary Daly in her study of the early years of the national school system in counties Cavan, Mayo, Cork and Kilkenny also discovered that a few individuals were responsible for a large number of schools.[23]

In that same study Mary Daly found that a high degree of continuity prevailed between the clerically patronised schools of the 1820s, as shown in the parochial returns of 1824, and the national schools of the 1830s.[24] If the same criteria are applied to county Meath the pattern is remarkably similar. As fig. 2.5 shows there is a high level of continuity between schools listed in the parochial returns of 1824 as receiving subscriptions from the parish, or schools listed as chapel schools, and the new emerging national schools.[25] Out of sixty such schools, thirty-eight of them, or sixty-three per cent are in parishes that had a national school by 1841. The Catholic clergy, aware of the increasing population and diminishing incomes, and faced with the task of church building, were not slow to take advantage of the opportunities for aid offered by the new system.

This is borne out by studying who the correspondents were for the seventy-eight national schools in 1841. The correspondent was the person with whom the board communicated regarding any school business. Sixty schools, or seventy-seven per cent of the total had priests as their correspondents. There were eighteen schools with lay correspondents. Five of these were lay Catholics, like Mr. Richard Ennis, the correspondent for both schools in Eden.[26] Two of the correspondents were the local landlords. Sir William Sommerville was the correspondent for both schools in Kentstown, and James Matthews was likewise for both schools in Kilshine at Mount Hanover.[27] Lord Killeen, a Catholic landowner, endowed both schools in Killeen.[28] Sir James Whiteside erected the school in Creewood.[29] Mr. F. Blundel, a factory owner at Athlumney, near Navan, built a school for the children of his workers and successfully applied for aid to the board in 1841. It became a national school and he became its correspondent.[30]

The commissioners gave aid towards the fitting up of school-houses with furniture, desks, books etc, and also towards the salary of teachers. They received applications for and granted aid towards the building of new school houses. A total of 108 applications for aid were received by the commissioners up to the end of 1841. Leaving out two of them which are no longer in the files, thirty-four sought aid for fitting up school-houses, thirty-six sought salary aid and thirty-two sought aid for building new school-houses. Four Poor Law Union schools, in Kells, Navan, Oldcastle and Trim, sought and received a grant of textbooks.[31] Very few applications were refused by the board. The figure of twenty-eight applications over and above the number of national schools in existence can be explained by the fact that some schools, like Culmullen, made more than one application for aid.[32] Other applications, like that of Cushenstown, were granted but the schools were not ready by the end of 1841.[33] The level of salary aid granted by the commissioners ranged from £5 to £10 in the early years but was increased to between £8 and £15 by 1840. William Downey, the teacher at Navan male national school, was paid £15 in 1840.[34] Considering that many teachers in the county in 1824 had an income in excess of £20 this was not very adequate.[35] However, it must be remembered that the commissioners expected the salaries of teachers to be supplemented at local level.

A study of the annual reports of the commissioners shows the level of aid granted to schools in county Meath. Their seventh report lists a total of twenty schools who had been granted aid but were not in operation up to 31 December 1840.[36] Table 2.2 outlines the level and type of aid granted.

Table 2.2

School	Building	Fitting up	Local aid	Year granted
Ballinabrackey Female & Ballinabrackey Male	£100	£11	£56	1840
Batterstown	£73		£37	1839
Bective Female & Bective Male	£100	£11	£56	1840
Carnisle	£140	£20	£80	1839
Castletown	£72	£10	£41	1838
Clonalvy Female & Clonalvy Male	£130	£10	£70	1839
Cormeen Female &				1839
Cormeen Male	£116	£8	£62	1839
Culmullen	£40		£20	1839
Kilcloon	£67	£8	£37	1840
Kilgriff	£80	£11	£46	1838
Kiltale	£90		£45	1837
Rathkenny Female & Rathkenny Male	£113		£56	1839
Stackallen	£230		£115	1834
Stamullen	£75	£10	£43	1839
Whitecross	£75	£10	£43	1839
Total	£1500	£109	£807	

According to the rules at least one third of the costs involved in the fitting up or building of a national school had to be raised locally. As table 2.2 shows this was adhered to in every one of these applications. A closer examination of the actual circumstances, however, can be made by check-ing the original application. In the case of Clonalvy the applicants requested £126 towards the completion of the schoolhouse whose cost they esti-mated at £186. The answer given to the question on local contribution was that they had no funds in hand but £20 had been donated in labour.[37] The applicants for Kilgriff school estimated the cost of their school at £150 'exclusive of a ceiling'. Fifty pounds had been pledged but not collected, but most people would contribute labour. They asked for aid of £100.[38] In her study, Mary Daly also found that much of the local contribution was accounted for by labour in kind.[39] The commissioners showed a certain flexibility in this regard.

It is not easy to gauge the effect that these schools had on the many other schools in existence, particularly the pay or hedge schools. It is clear from the applications that many of the latter were held in contempt by some locals. The application from Moynalty lists seven other schools in the country areas of the parish and describes them as 'very inferior and not in any connection with a society.'[40] Likewise, the application for aid towards a new school-house at Stamullen paints a gloomy picture 'Nothing in the parish except a miserable hedge school at Tullogue, two and a half miles south west of Stamullen, and another equally wretched one at Lisdornan, two and a quarter miles north west'.[41] Fr. John O' Connell, the parish priest of Kildalkey applying for aid to the board in 1834 remarked that:

> It is intended to build a new school at Carnisle. There are five small schools in different parts of the parish, which would immediately cease to exist if the teachers at Kildalkey school were enabled to teach the poor gratis.[42]

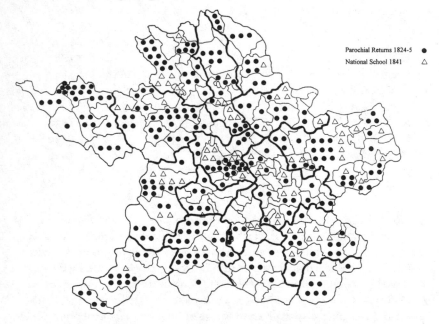

Figure 2.6 Map showing the distribution of schools in county Meath, as outlined in the parochial returns of 1824-5 and also the distribution of national schools in 1841.

Figure 2.7 Map showing the type and distribution of schools in county Meath, according to the Royal Commission on Public Instruction in 1835.

While applicants for aid cannot be seen as totally disinterested observers, their information on the poor physical quality of the hedge or pay schools is supported by evidence from the parochial returns of 1824-5.[43]

Figure 2.6 compares the distribution of schools as found in the parochial returns of 1824 with the distribution of national schools in 1841.[44] The pattern that emerges is not unexpected. The largest concentration of national schools are to be found in areas of the county which had a large number of schools in 1824.

More informative is fig. 2.7 which maps the distribution of schools in the county in 1834. The source for this information is the report of the Royal Commission on public instruction in Ireland which was published in 1835.[45] It found twenty-three national schools in the county, twenty-nine parish or free schools and 171 hedge or pay schools. All told there were 223 schools, which represents a drop of nineteen per cent on the 1824-5 figure of 277 schools. Figure 2.7 would seem to indicate that in areas where a national school existed there was a fall in the number of other schools as against the situation in 1824. Moynalty in the north west of the county, and Dunboyne in the south east are good examples of this. Thus, as early as 1834, national schools were beginning to supplant the pay schools.

Mention has already been made of a high level of continuity between chapel and subscription schools and the emerging national schools. In fact the schools which made the transition from pay schools to national schools were invariably those established by a local priest or landlord. Out of a total of sixty chapel schools, or schools supported by subscription, thirty-one or 51.6 per cent made this transition. The percentage is even higher if schools like Killeen, which was supported by the local landlord, are included. Its application for aid shows that it was in existence as early as 1813.[46]

Further evidence of the continuity between national schools and the pay schools emerges from an examination of the early teachers whose salaries were paid by the commissioners. At least twenty of the applications state that the teachers had previous experience. James Curran, the teacher in Donore was said to have had twenty-four years' teaching experience.[47] Even more solid evidence emerges if the salary books of the commissioners are examined and the teachers names compared with those who were listed as teaching in 1824-5 by the parochial returns. There were sixty-two teachers being paid by the board in 1840 and of these, twenty-nine or forty-seven per cent were teaching in 1824-5.[48] Seventeen of these teachers were still teaching in the same school as they had in 1824-5. It is not possible to make a comparison with the 1824-5 report for all schools in the county. Although the 1835 report of the royal commission on the state of public instruction lists all the schools in the county it only names the teachers in sixty-nine schools. Of these teachers, twenty-one can be traced back to 1824-5, and sixteen are in the same schools.

Most of these existing schools that became national schools were found to be in good repair by the inspector who called to inspect them for the board. In the early years the inspectors spent much time assessing the applications for aid on behalf of the board. The inspector in the Meath area was Michael Coyle. His reports which became part of the applications are very interesting and they provide a great deal of information not only on the schools but also on the teachers and the community in general. He found the school in Cortown, on 28 June 1841, to be in excellent repair. It was 'Mud and stone, thatched, consisting of two rooms, both 19 x 15 x 8.5 ft, in excellent repair with three tables and six forms in each room'.[49] The application, not surprisingly, sought aid in the form of a teacher's salary and a grant of textbooks. The school in Grangegeeth was built by 'the manager [Fr. Nicholas Duff] and his friends in expectation of aid from the board'.[50] The school at Yellow Furze on 10 December, 1840, was also in excellent repair, being new, and built of lime and stone and thatched with two fireplaces. Its furnishings, however, left a lot to be desired, consisting of 'poor furniture, a few old forms and planks along the walls'.[51]

A few schools like Castletown were not in good repair. In his report, following his visit there in September 1841, Michael Coyle recommended that as it had been allocated a grant of aid, a new schoolhouse should be provided as soon as possible.[52] After his visit to Killeen on 8 October 1836 the correspondent was written to and informed of the 'discreditable state of the school' and was urged to build a new school. After his visit on the 21 April 1837 he described the school as 'an objectionable house in every respect.'[53] His reports on the teachers in these schools are generally favourable. There was a shortage of trained teachers in the early years and many teachers were like Bartholemew Lynch in Fraine school, near Athboy, who had 'no formal training, just the usual country mode.'[54] Margaret Carey, the teacher in Duleek female school had never conducted school before but was 'capable of becoming a good teacher. Her knowledge is limited at present ... but she just needs instruction.'[55]

Likewise, Michael Fallon in Bohermeen had never taught before but was qualified to teach reading, writing, grammar, arithmetic and euclid. His method of conducting the school was not up to par as 'he does not conduct it judiciously, but a little instruction will enable him to do so.'[56] Simon Kindelan in Longwood conducted the school in a manner which was 'not bad considering the circumstances'.[57] Michael McDermott in Mullahea school, near Kells, was highly commended indeed. He was, 'excellent in character and well qualified. He knows english grammar, geography and arithmetic. He reads well and conducts the school industriously and judiciously'.[58] One of the reasons given for recommending aid for a separate female school in Duleek was that the male teacher was 'not qualified to teach females' as he could not handle needlework.[59] Michael Coyle was very much in favour of separate schooling for girls. In recommending aid for a female school in Bohermeen in September 1842 he remarked that:

> The male teacher could not teach all the children of both sexes that attend even if the male school could accommodate them and there is a second separate room for the females to which the male teacher could not attend. Besides, where a good mistress can be procured, such as I consider the person named herein to be, females derive more advantage as to manners, tidiness, and neatness from her instruction, than from that of a male teacher, and without improvement in these points a knowledge of reading, writing, etc can benefit them very little.[60]

If he was in favour of separate instruction for girls, he certainly did not approve of unequal pay for teachers. When he inspected Moynalty school in April 1836 he complained that the manager: 'divides the salary unjustly, giving the master £8 and the mistress £12, the latter not having one third of the children and having apartments'.[61] Unequal pay was not the only difficulty he met on his inspections. On a visit to Carlanstown national school in April 1836 the teacher Thomas Wallace could not 'reply to him for effect of drinking'. It was supposed to be 'accidental but said to be habitual.' The correspondent was written to on the matter but replied that from 'his own opinion, and that of the character given by the Protestant clergyman who states he never heard of anything discreditable of the teacher, he thought well of him'. Wallace was fined £1 but the difficulty persisted and he was dismissed in June 1837.[62]

Some schools like Walterstown had serious problems with teachers. On 1 December 1835 the teacher John Clarke was dismissed for drunkenness and replaced by Nicholas Fagan. But when it was inspected in September 1836 it was found to be almost deserted. The correspondent was written to and replied that he had appointed another master, Patrick Cosgrave in March 1837. The school was inspected in July 1837 and a favourable report was written. However, by October, Cosgrave had been dismissed on foot of an inspector's report for drunkenness. Despite appealing for clemency to the board he was not re-instated. The new teacher, Matthew Henry resigned on 20 May 1840.[63]

The applications and inspectors reports are a very rich source of information not only on teachers but on the wider community as well. The report on the school in Clonard school in November 1836 stated that although it was four years in connection with the board it was 'not creditable.' Part of the difficulty had to do with the death of the teacher and his son from cholera.[64] The application from Fraine school, near Athboy described the local population. 'They hold from thirty to two acres. Many live on the edge of the bog. The late census puts the population at 962 persons.'[65] The application from Duleek female school in 1841 outlined that the local population was 'very numerous' and consisted mainly of 'small shopkeepers, artisans, landholders, and labourers, all of them poor.'[66] Duleek male school was only the third in the county to apply for aid to the commissioners. The community was described as 'A large population in the village consisting of weavers and labourers who have little employment and even this badly paid, and whose children, three hundred of them, are in need of education'.[67] Michael Coyle found the population of the area around Newton school to be 'seventeen hundred persons most of them comfortable, small farmers or work as labourers, all uneducated ... The neglected state of education in the locality is a reproach to the clergy and gentry of the neighbourhood'.[68] The local population in the vicinity of Stackallen school consisted of 'four hundred families, 2,000 people, with some Protestant families but no sectarian differences'.[69] There is plenty of evidence in the applications that relations between the Catholic and Protestant communities were quite harmonious.

The requirement to have applications signed by members of both communities posed no difficulty. The application from Ashbourne in 1835 contained twenty-three Catholic signatures and seven Protestant ones.[70] The Killeen application had thirteen Catholic and five Protestant signatures.[71] There were some difficulties, as is shown by the application from Cloghan sent in by Fr. John Langan, parish priest of Duleek, 'there are but two Protestants in the parish, one of them illiterate, and the other an unfortunate profligate. As for the Protestant rector, Rev. Mr. Batty, he has refused to sign for Duleek school, he therefore shall not be troubled by me'.[72] In 1841 sixty national schools had local Catholic clergy as their correspondents. All of these clergy and more besides had signed applications for aid to the commissioners. The reaction of the Anglican clergy was almost entirely hostile to the new system. Out of thirty-nine Anglican clergy mentioned in the first 108 applications to the board only three of them signed applications. In the case of all the others they are recorded in the applications as being in varying degrees hostile to the new system. The application from Dunshaughlin states that:

> the Rev. George Irvine, rector of the parish has declined, as has the Rev. Henry Liddiard of Knockmark glebe. The other parson within a reasonable distance Rev. William Irvine [father of the Dunshaughlin rector] of Killeen glebe. Norman of Ratoath and Matthews of Kilheggan [*sic*] are well known to be hostile to the board.[73]

The three Protestant and twelve Catholic applicants from Doneycarney in 1839 claimed the local rector was 'a person whose religious and political feelings are of so exclusive a cast that we did not wish to subject ourselves to a refusal by applying to him for a signature'.[74] Some of the Anglican clergy gave reasons why they would not co-operate. The vicar of Kilmainhamwood, the Rev. Thomas Foster refused to sign in 1835 as he might 'incur the displeasure of his bishop.'[75] The local Anglican clergyman refused to sign the application for Mullahea school in 1841 because he would not 'consent to any school that prohibits the full, free and unrestricted use of the Holy Scriptures.'[76]

The Rev. Robert Noble, rector of Athboy, was stated in the application from Rathcarne in 1840 to have said that he 'thought a school was necessary but as there were few of his people there he would not interfere.'[77] This same clergyman was mentioned in the evidence given to the House of Lords inquiry into the new system of education in 1837 by the Rev. B.W. Noel. He said that in one case he had heard of a clergyman who objected to the new system but still thought it his duty to do what he could to improve the national school in his area by visiting it.

> What was the effect in the school? He said that at first his visits were viewed with jealousy; that had subsided; but he had seen no particu-

lar effect. In what county was that? That was the clergyman of Athboy.
Did you visit that school? I did not. Can you state the clergyman's
name? Mr. Noble.[78]

The three Anglican clergymen who signed applications were the Rev. Joseph
Stevenson for Newtown school, the Rev. Brabason W. Disney for Stackallen
school, and the Rev. William Kellett for both the male and female schools
in Moynalty.[79]

It is an interesting social commentary that so many Protestants were
willing to sign the applications despite the strong disapproval of the new
system by their clergy. It has to be said however that while they may have
signed the applications they did not send their children to these schools. As
will be seen later, the new system became an almost entirely denominational system.

A question that arises out of the applications is who were the lay signatories? Mention has been made elsewhere about the fact that there was little
difficulty in obtaining a mixture of Catholic and Protestants who were willing to sign applications. The majority of applications were initiated by the
Catholic clergy but what kind of people did they approach? The applications do not give much information on these people, no occupation is
given except for clergy or doctors. If however, they are compared with the
tithe applotment books for the period and Pigot's commercial directory
some information does emerge. Table 2.3 lists the signatories for Moynalty
and Navan and gives their valuation and/or occupation as found in the tithe
applotment books and Pigot.[80]

A number of those who signed the Moynalty applications were large
landowners, and if some of the Navan signatories were less well endowed
with property, there were still some prominent business people. The same
pattern is repeated elsewhere. The application from Dunboyne school in
1835 contained no Protestant signatures but had ten Catholic ones, most of
whom had a property valuation between £90 and £350.[81] Mary Daly in
her study also found that the greater number of signatories or school trustees
were gentlemen or businessmen.[82]

Surprisingly, given that the whole system was set up for their benefit,
there is little information in the applications on the pupils who attended
these national schools. Unlike the parochial returns of 1824 there is no
breakdown given in the applications or the commissioners reports on the
religious affiliation of the children. There is such a breakdown in the 1837
report of the House of Lords inquiry. Out of the forty-two national schools
mentioned in the report, ten gave a religious breakdown of the pupils.
These schools on the day of inspection had seventeen Protestant pupils and
1,191 Catholic pupils.[83] It is unclear why the other schools did not give a
similar breakdown. The picture however, is of an overwhelmingly denomi-

Name	Occupation	Valuation
MOYNALTY		
Protestant signatures		
William Kellett	Rector	£50
Robert Kellett		£157
William Garnett		
Samuel Bland		
Joseph Bland		
William Rathbourne	Church warden	
George Garnett		
James Hillett	Church warden	
Catholic signatures		
Philip Farrelly	Parish priest	
Peter Ham	Catholic curate	
Patrick Masterson		£140
Patrick Reilly		£6
James Farrelly		
John Farrell		£157
NAVAN		
Protestant Signatures		
James Morgan	Corn merchant	£51
Thomas Williams		
Thomas Moore		
Thomas Christian		
Catholic Signatures		
Patrick Clarke		£557
John Leonard		£6
Peter Commons		
George Legg		
Patrick Murray		
Andrew Ryan	Publican	
Peter Sherlock	Chandler	£3
Robert Russell	Watchmaker	
Nicholas Russell		£7
Patrick Martin		£2
James Guggerty		£3

Table 2.3

national school system. Ironically, by refusing to co-operate with the new board the established church ensured the development of a denominational education system in the country.

The numbers of pupils in the system grew each year as the number of schools increased throughout the county. What emerges clearly from the enrollment figures is an increase in the numbers of females being educated by 1841. The number of females in Moynalty national school grew from forty-one per cent of the total enrollment in 1835 to fifty-six per cent of enrollment in 1841.[84] The percentage of females attending Duleek school grew in the same period from thirty per cent to forty per cent. Parents were now more inclined to send their female children to school as the tuition was free. Overall figures for the county show an increase from forty-one per cent in 1835 to forty-four per cent in 1841. By 1850 the figures were almost fifty per cent.

The applications to the commissioners and their annual reports provide a great deal of information on the early years of the national school system in county Meath and on the players involved in it, the teachers, applicants, pupils and indeed the wider community. The expansion in the number of schools and pupils is evidence of significant achievement. The national schools did not mark a sudden discontinuity with the past, in many cases existing schools and teachers continued with a new source of finance. But just as in the case of aid for schools from the proselytising societies in the period up to the early 1830s there is evidence to show that only the more prosperous areas of the county were to benefit in the initial stages of the system up to 1841. The vast majority of pay or hedge schools, however, were either not able or not willing to take advantage of the new possibilities offered. Eventually they would disappear completely beneath the tide of an ever expanding national system.

Conclusion

This study has shown what level of educational provision existed in county Meath in the mid 1820s and how it was affected by the advent of the new national system in 1831. It was the inadequacy of the existing system, particularly for the Catholic population, which led to the commission of inquiry in 1824. The remarkable survey, reproduced in its second report, provides a snapshot of educational provisional in the county in the period 1824-5. It indicates that there were a great variety of schools in the county but they were not capable of catering for the large numbers of children who could not afford to pay for their tuition. The Protestant parish schools and a few of the Catholic free schools were fairly well resourced but the vast majority of schools were inadequate to the task that was necessary. That there was a great desire for education is shown by the efforts made especially by the Catholic population to educate their children. Their ability to do so depended very much on their economic well being. The more economically prosperous areas of the county were better able to provide schools and pay for their children's education. The situation in county Meath indicates that the concerns about education being expressed at a national level by Catholic politicians and the Irish hierarchy were valid.

The new national system of education was availed of almost immediately in parts of the county. As shown in other local areas, there was in county Meath a high level of continuity between the more well established chapel schools or schools supported by parish subscription and the new national schools. In many instances existing schools and teachers continued as national schools. The system was a welcome relief to Catholic parishes trying to cope with expanding population and economic distress, and it provided their existing schools with a new and regular source of finance. There was an increase in enrollment but it is unclear whether these children in the early years of the system were switching allegiance from hedge schools or were attending school for the first time.

Two points in particular emerge from this study. Firstly, it is remarkable the extent to which the local perspective mirrors the national one in this area of education. The exact concerns being voiced at a national level can be seen operating at the local level, whether it be demands for some measure of educational reform in the 1820s or opposition from the established church to the new system that was set up. Secondly, the issue of schooling cannot be separated from the local community and its economic well being.

More prosperous areas of the county were able to take advantage of the new national system more quickly because they could afford the one third local contribution. Later, when this regulation was relaxed, the national schools spread more widely. It is not possible to take the county in isolation, because within the county there were important regional variations.

In all that has been written in this study of education in county Meath the picture that should not be lost sight of is that of a community struggling to live and exist in what for many of them were very difficult circumstances. A community made up of parents grasping at opportunities to make a better life for their children, teachers living and working, inspectors trying to do their job, priests attempting to cater for the needs of their parishioners, and Anglican clergy fearing the loss of their influence in society.

'If men could learn from history, what lessons it might teach us! But passion and party blind our eyes, and the light which experience gives is a lantern on the stern, which shines only on the waves behind us!'

(Samuel T. Coleridge).

Notes

ABBREVIATIONS

Throughout this study all footnotes to parliamentary papers include the printed pagination and the manuscript pagination, eg. *Appendix to the fourteenth report from the commissioners of the board of education in Ireland*, p. 15 (= printed pagination), H.C. 1812-13 (21), vi, p. 235 (= manuscript pagination).

The only exception to this rule is for the following parliamentary paper for which I was unable to find a manuscript pagination: *Appendix to the second report of the commissioners of Irish education inquiry* (Parochial Abstracts), pp. 724-49, H.C. 1826-7 (12), xii.

As frequent use is made of this particular parliamentary paper in the text, especially in Chapter 1, it is not always footnoted. Wherever 'parochial returns' are mentioned, it should be taken as a reference to this paper.

INTRODUCTION

1 Mary Daly, 'The development of the national education system 1831-1840', in Art Cosgrove and Donal Mc Cartney (eds), *Studies in Irish History* (Dublin, 1979), pp. 151-63; Harold O'Sullivan, 'The emergence of the national system of education in north county Louth (Diocese of Armagh)', in *County Louth Archaeological and Historical Journal*, xviii (1973), pp. 7-37; Sr. Mary Fahy, *Education in the diocese of Kilmacduagh in the nineteenth century* (Gort, 1972); J.P. Kelly, 'The national system of education in Connaught, 1831-1870', unpublished M.A. thesis, University College Dublin, 1975; W. Boyle, 'National education in Co. Donegal, 1831-1901', unpublished M.A. thesis, St. Patrick's College, Maynooth, 1990; Claire Cotter, 'The development of primary education in county Carlow, 1820-1870', unpublished M. Ed thesis, St. Patrick's College, Maynooth, 1991.

2 J.P. Kelly, 'The national system of education in Connaught, 1831-1870'; Boyle, 'National education in Donegal'; Cotter, 'The development of primary education in county Carlow'.

EDUCATION IN CO. MEATH
1824-5

1 *Hansard 2*, xl, 837-47, 9th March 1824.
2 *Hansard 2*, xl, 1399-1413, 25 March 1824.
3 *First report of the commissioners of Irish education inquiry*, pp. 1-881, H.C. 1825 (400), xii, pp. 1-997; *Second report ...* pp. 1-1331, H.C. 1826-7 (12), xii; *Third report ...* pp. 3-32, H.C. 1826-7 (13), xiii, pp. 1-155; *Fourth report ...* pp. 3-202, H.C. 1826-7 (89), xiii, pp. 156-358; *Fifth report ...* pp. 3-26, H.C. 1826-7 (441), xiii, pp. 359-84; *Sixth report ...* pp. 3-116, H.C. 1826-7 (442), xiii, pp. 385-500; *Seventh report ...* pp. 3-36, H.C. 1826-7 (443), xiii, pp. 501-36; *Eighth report ...* pp. 3- 461, H.C. 1826-7 (509), xiii, pp. 537-998; *Ninth report ...* pp. 3-138, H.C. 1826-7 (516), xiii, pp. 1001-1131.
4 *Appendix to the second report of the commissioners of Irish education inquiry* (Parochial Abstracts) pp. 724-49, H.C. 1826-7 (12), xii.
5 *Appendix to the second report of the commissioners of Irish education inquiry* (Parochial Abstracts) p. 1, H.C. 1826-7 (12), xii.

6   *Appendix to the second report of the commis-sioners of Irish education inquiry* (Parochial Abstracts) p. 34, H.C. 1826-7 (12), xii.

7   *Abstract of answers and returns pursuant to the act for taking account of the population of Ire-land, enumeration abstract*, appendix, pp. 80-90 H.C. 1824 (577,1823), xxii, pp. 513-25.

8   *Abstract of answers and returns pursuant to the act for taking account of the population of Ire-land, enumeration abstract*, appendix, p. 232, H.C. 1824 (577,1823), xxii, p. 666.

9   Sir Henry Piers, *A chorographical description of the county of Meath* (Tara, 1981), p. 112.

10   Timothy Corcoran, *Education systems in Ire-land, from the close of the middle Ages* (Dub-lin, 1928), pp. 51-6.

11   Rev. William Burke, *The Irish priests in the penal times* (Waterford, 1914), p. 396.

12   21 and 22 George III, c. 62. s. 1.

13   Anthony Cogan, *The ecclesiastical history of the diocese of Meath, ancient and modern* (3 vols, Dublin, 1862-7, reprinted Dublin 1992), iii, pp. 86-7.

14   Cogan, *Ecclesiastical history of the diocese of Meath*, iii, pp. 87-8.

15   32 George III, c 21

16   Patrick Dowling, *The hedge schools of Ire-land* (London, 1935), p. 31.

17   Fr. John Brady, Unpublished notes on the history of St. Finian's College, Mullingar, St. Finian's College archives.

18   Fr. John Brady, *A short history of the par-ishes of the diocese of Meath, 1870-1940* (Navan, 1940), Navan, p. 101.

19   Cogan, *Ecclesiastical history of the diocese of Meath*, iii, p. 136.

20   Cogan, *Ecclesiastical history of the diocese of Meath*, ii, pp. 202-10.

21   28 Henry VIII, c.15.

22   12 Elizabeth c. I.

23   Dowling, *The hedge schools of Ireland*, pp. 33-4.

24   Hugh Boulter, *Letters written by His Excel-lency Hugh Boulter, D.D. Lord Primate of All Ireland etc,to several ministers of state in England and some others, containing an account of the most interesting transactions, which passed in Ireland from 1724 to 1738* (2 vols, Ox-ford, 1769-70), ii, p. 10.

25   Edward Wakefield, *An account of Ireland statistical and political* (2 vols, London, 1812), ii, pp. 411-12.

26   *Fourth report of the commissioners of the board of education in Ireland* (Diocesan Free Schools), pp. 1-5, H.C. 1810 (174) x, pp. 209-13; *Eleventh report of the commissioners of the board of education in Ireland* (Parish Schools), pp. 1-9, H.C. 1810-11 (107), vi, pp. 927-35.

27   *First report of the commissioners of Irish educa-tion inquiry*, app, p. 15, H.C. 1825 (400), xii, p. 131.

28   Dowling, *The hedge schools of Ireland*, p. 45.

29   Brady, *History of the parishes of the diocese of Meath*, Longwood. p. 78.

30   *Appendix to the second report of the commis-sioners of Irish education inquiry* (Parochial Abstracts), p. 18, H.C. 1826-7 (12), xii.

31   *Appendix to the fourteenth report from the com-missioners of the board of education in Ireland*, p. 15, H.C. 1812-13 (21), vi, p. 235.

32   Donald Akenson, *The Irish education ex-periment – the national system of education in the nineteenth century* (London, 1970), pp. 81-2.

33   Akenson, *Irish education experiment*, p. 85; for payment of teachers see Brady, *History of the parishes of the diocese of Meath*, Moyn-alty pp. 265-7, Nobber p. 274.

34   *First report of the commissioners of Irish educa-tion inquiry*, p. 66, H.C. 1825 (400) xii, p. 70.

35   *First report of the commissioners of Irish educa-tion inquiry*, p. 67, H.C. 1825 (400) xii, p. 71.

36   Akenson, *Irish education experiment*, pp. 85-6.

37   National Archives, Official Papers, O.P. 693.

38   National Archives, Official Papers, O.P. 693.

39   Akenson, *Irish education experiment*, pp. 86-7.

40   Mary Daly, 'The development of the na-tional school system, 1831-1840', in Art Cosgrove, Donal Mc Cartney (eds), *Stud-ies in Irish History*, p. 152.

41   National Archives, ED 1/66.

42   Akenson, *Irish education experiment*, p. 83.

43   Brady, *History of the parishes of the diocese of Meath*, Moynalty, p. 265

44   Church of Ireland College of Education Library, Records of the Kildare Place So-ciety, MS 358, No. 11.

45 Church of Ireland College of Education Library, Records of the Kildare Place Society, MS 358, No. 203.

46 Brady, *History of the parishes of the diocese of Meath*, Oldcastle, pp. 474-5.

47 National Archives, ED 1/66.

48 National Archives, ED 1/66-29.

49 Brady, *History of the parishes of the diocese of Meath*, Rathmolyon, p. 189.

50 Brady, *History of the parishes of the diocese of Meath*, Kilskyre, p. 462.

51 Akenson, *Irish education experiment*, pp. 378-84.

52 Brady, *History of the parishes of the diocese of Meath*, Kells, p. 135.

53 Peter Connell, 'An economic geography of Co. Meath 1770-1870', St. Patrick's College Maynooth, unpublished M.A. thesis, 1980, p. 28.

54 John Mc Call, *Manuscript history of Irish almanacks*, quoted in Brady, *History of the parishes of the diocese of Meath*, Kells, p. 135.

55 Peter Galligan, Unpublished Manuscript, quoted in Dowling, *Hedge schools of Ireland*, pp. 150-1.

56 W.E. Vaughan, A.J. Fitzpatrick, *Irish historical statistics – population 1821-1970* (Dublin, 1978), p. xii.

57 *Abstract of answers and returns pursuant to the act for taking account of the population of Ireland, enumeration abstract*, appendix, p. 94, H.C. 1824 (577, 1823), xxii, p. 528.

58 Church of Ireland College of Education Library, Records of the Kildare Place Society, MS 358, No 133.

59 Church of Ireland College of Education Library, Records of the Kildare Place Society, MS 358, No 170.

60 Royal Irish Academy, Halliday Collection, quoted in Brady, *History of the parishes of the diocese of Meath*, Bohermeen, p. 115.

61 Brady, *History of the parishes of the diocese of Meath*, Kilskyre, p. 463.

62 Brady, *History of the parishes of the diocese of Meath*, Moynalty, pp. 265-7.

63 Brady, *History of the parishes of the diocese of Meath*, Nobber, p. 274.

64 Brady, *History of the parishes of the diocese of Meath*, Trim, p. 206.

65 Dowling, *Hedge schools of Ireland*, p. 150.

66 *Second report of the commissioners of public instruction*, Ireland, p. 144, H.C. 1835, xxxiv, p. 163.

67 *Second report of the commissioners of public instruction*, Ireland, p. 155, H.C. 1835, xxxiv, p. 174.

68 Connell, 'An economic geography of Co. Meath 1770-1870', pp. 17-27.

69 T. Jones Hughes, 'Landholding in Meath and Cavan', in Patrick O'Flanagan, Paul Ferguson, Kevin Whelan (eds), *Rural Ireland, modernisation and change, 1600-1900* (Cork, 1987), pp. 127-9.

70 Mr. & Mrs S.C. Hall, *Ireland, its Scenery, Character, Etc.* (London, 1842), p. 373.

THE DEVELOPMENT OF THE NATIONAL SCHOOL SYSTEM IN CO. MEATH, 1831-41

1 *Hansard* 3, vi, 1249-305.

2 Donald Akenson, *The Irish education experiment – the national system of education in the nineteenth century* (London, 1970), pp. 114-15.

3 Ambrose Macaulay, *William Crolly, archbishop of Armagh 1835-49* (Dublin, 1994), p. 147.

4 *Reports of the commissioners of national education in Ireland – from the year 1834 to 1845 inclusive, Vol I* (Dublin, 1851), pp. 1-5.

5 John Coolahan, 'The daring first decade of the board of national education, 1831-1841', in *The Irish Journal of Education*, xvii, 1, (1983), pp. 40-1.

6 *Appendix to the twelfth report of the commissioners of national education in Ireland, for the year 1845*, p. 16 [711] H.C. 1846, xxii, p. 326.

7 *Fourteenth report of the commissioners of national education in Ireland, for the year 1847*, p. 27 [981], H.C. 1847-8, xvii, p. 245.

8 Minutes of the board meetings of the commissioners of national education in Ireland, National Library of Ireland, MS 5529, Vol A, 1/1/1831 to 16/2/1837.

9 Coolahan, 'The daring first decade of the board of national education', p. 35.

10 *Report of the select committee of the House of Lords on the plan of education in Ireland, with minutes of evidence*, pt i, pp. 1-743, H.C. 1837 (543-I), viii, pp. 1-749, pt ii, pp. 744-1491, H.C. 1837 (543-II), viii, pp. 1-753; *Report from the select committee appointed to inquire into the progress and operation of the*

new plan of education in Ireland, pp. 1-694, H.C. 1837 (485), ix, pp. 1-760; *Report from the select committee on foundation schools and education in Ireland*, pp. 1-92, H.C. 1837-8 [701], vii, pp. 345-436.

11 Akenson, *Irish education experiment*, p. 321.

12 National Archives, ED 1/66, No. 1.

13 National Archives, ED 1/66, No. 23.

14 National Archives, ED 1/66.

15 National Archives ED 1/66; *Reports of the commissioners of national education in Ireland, second eighth reports, 1835-41*.

16 Emmet Larkin, 'The quarrel among the Roman Catholic hierarchy over the national system of education in Ireland 1838-41', in R. B. Browne, Roscilli et al. (eds), *The Celtic cross* (Perdue, 1964), pp. 121-46.

17 *Appendix to the second report of the commissioners of Irish education inquiry (Parochial Abstracts)*, pp. 724-49, H.C. 1826-7 (12), xii; *Second report of the commissioners of national education in Ireland, for the year ending 31st March 1835*, pp. 38-9, H.C. 1835 [300], xxxv, pp. 72-3; *Third report ... for the year ending 31st March 1836*, pp. 40-1 [44], H.C. 1836, xxxvi, pp. 136-7; *Fourth report ... for the year ending 31st March 1837*, p. 23 [110], H.C. 1837-8, xxviii, p. 71; *Fifth report ... for the year ending 31st March 1838*, pp. 54-7 [160], H.C. 1839, xvi, pp. 398-401; *Sixth report ... for the year 1839*, pp. 55-7 [246], H.C. 1840, xxviii, pp. 103-5; *Seventh report ... for the year 1840*, pp. 73-4 [353], H.C. 1842, xxiii, pp. 289-90; *Eighth report ...for the year 1841*, pp. 79-82 [398], H.C. 1842, xxiii, pp. 417-20.

18 W.E. Vaughan, A.J. Fitzpatrick, *Irish Historical Statistics-population 1821-1971* (Dublin, 1978), p. 106.

19 *Second report of the commissioners of public instruction, Ireland*, pp. 106-56 (47) H.C. 1835, xxxiv, pp. 124-74.

20 *Report of the commissioners appointed to take the census of Ireland for the year 1841* (Dublin, 1843), p. 94.

21 *Second report of the commissioners of public instruction, Ireland*, p. 135 (47) H.C. 1835, xxxiv, p. 154.

22 National Archives, ED 1/66.

23 Mary Daly, 'The development of the national school system, 1831-1840', in Art

24 Daly, 'Development of the national school system', p. 156.

25 *Appendix to the second report of the commissioners of Irish education inquiry* (Parocial Abstracts), pp. 724-49, H.C. 1826-7 (12), xii.

26 National Archives, ED1/66, No. 36.

27 National Archives, ED1/66, No. 56 (Kentstown), No. 27 (Mt. Hanover).

28 National Archives, ED1/66, Nos. 10 & 47.

29 National Archives, ED 1/66, No. 91.

30 National Archives, ED 1/66, No. 68.

31 National Archives, ED 1/66.

32 National Archives, ED 1/66, Nos. 16 & 50.

33 National Archives, ED 1/66, No. 84.

34 National Archives, ED 4/4, Salary Books, 1839-40, Co. Meath.

35 *Appendix to the second report of the commissioners of Irish education inquiry* (Parochial Abstracts), pp. 724-49, H.C. 1826-7 (12), xii.

36 *Seventh report of the commissioners of national education in Ireland, for the year 1840*, pp. 73-4 [353], H.C. 1842, xxiii, pp. 289-90.

37 National Archives, ED 1/66, No. 57.

38 National Archives, ED 1/66, No. 40.

39 Daly, 'The development of the national school system', p. 155.

40 National Archives, ED 1/66, No. 17.

41 National Archives, ED 1/66, No. 59.

42 National Archives, ED 1/66, No. 29.

43 *Appendix to the second report of the commissioners of Irish education inquiry* (Parochial Abstracts), pp. 724-49, H.C. 1826-7 (12), xii.

44 *Appendix to the second report of the commissioners of Irish education inquiry* (Parochial Abstracts), pp. 724-49, H.C. 1826-7 (12), xii.

45 *Second report of the commissioners of public instruction, Ireland*, pp. 106-56 (47) H.C. 1835, xxxiv, pp. 124-74.

46 National Archives, ED 1/66, No. 56.

47 National Archives, ED 1/66, No. 13.

48 National Archives, ED 4/4; *Appendix to the second report of the commissioners of Irish education inquiry* (Parochial Abstracts) pp. 724-49, H.C. 1826-7, (12), xii.

49 National Archives, ED 1/66, No. 79.

Cosgrove, Donal McCartney (eds), *Studies in Irish History* (Dublin, 1979), p. 159.

50 National Archives, ED 1/66, No. 72.

51 National Archives, ED 1/66, No. 73.

52 National Archives, ED 1/66, No. 87.

53 National Archives, ED 2/34, Register, Co. Meath, No. 10 – Killeen school.

54 National Archives, ED 1/66, No. 9.

55 National Archives, ED 1/66, No. 78.

56 National Archives, ED 1/66, No. 77.

57 National Archives, ED 1/66, No. 93.

58 National Archives, ED 1/66, No. 69.

59 National Archives, ED 1/66, No. 78.

60 National Archives, ED 1/66, No. 107.

61 National Archives, ED 2/34, Register, Co. Meath, No. 18 – Moynalty school.

62 National Archives, ED 2/34, Register, Co. Meath, No. 7 – Carlanstown school.

63 National Archives, ED 2/34, Register, Co. Meath, No. 20 – Walterstown school.

64 National Archives, ED 2/34, Register, Co. Meath, No. 9 – Clonard school.

65 National Archives, ED 1/66, No. 11.

66 National Archives, ED 1/66, No. 78.

67 National Archives, ED 1/66, No. 3.

68 National Archives, ED 1/66, No. 96.

69 National Archives, ED 1/66, No. 26.

70 National Archives, ED 1/66, No. 24.

71 National Archives, ED 1/66, No. 10.

72 National Archives, ED 1/66, No. 51.

73 National Archives, ED 1/66, No. 42.

74 National Archives, ED 1/66, No. 53.

75 National Archives, ED 1/66, No. 36.

76 National Archives, ED 1/66, No. 69.

77 National Archives, ED 1/66, No 66.

78 *Report of the select committee of the House of Lords on the plan of education in Ireland; with minutes of evidence*, pt i, pp. 1-743, H.C. 1837 (543-1), vii, pp. 1-749, pt ii, pp. 744-1491, H.C. 1837, (543-II), viii, pp. 1-753.

79 National Archives, ED 1/66, No. 80 (Newtown), No 26 (Stackallen), Nos. 17 & 18 (Moynalty).

80 National Archives, Tithe Applotment Books, Co. Meath, Navan 22/78, Moynaty 22/77; Pigot & Co., *City of Dublin and Hibernian Provincial Directory* (Dublin, 1824), pp. 175-6; National Archives ED 1/66, No. 1 (Navan), No. 17 (Moynalty).

81 National Archives, ED 1/66 No. 35.

82 Mary Daly, 'The development of the national school system', p. 156.

83 *Report of the select committee of the House of Lords on the plan of education in Ireland; with minutes of evidence*, pt i, pp. 1-743, H.C. 1837 (543-1), viii, pp. 1-749, pt ii, pp. 744-1491, H.C. 1837 (543-1), viii, pp. 1-753.

84 *Second report of the commissioners of national education in Ireland, for the year ending 31st March 1835*, pp. 38-9, H.C. 1835 [300], xxxv, pp. 72-3; *Eighth report … for the year ending 1841*, pp. 79-82 [398], H.C. 1842, xxiii, pp. 417-20.